"Enlightenment for an everyday person like m[...] shows us that awakening can be found not on[...] This much-needed set of beautifully written, relatable, and [...] teachings helps those of us living in the real world learn how freedom is found right at home. If the Real Housewives of Buddhism had a book on their nightstand, it would be *Real-World Enlightenment*."

—Sumi Loundon Kim, Buddhist chaplain, Yale University, and author of *Sitting Together*

"*Real-World Enlightenment* is a roadmap for anyone asking, 'How can I lead a more meaningful life?' Weaving together Buddhist wisdom, literary insights, and personal anecdotes, Susan Kaiser Greenland takes enlightenment down from the pedestal and empowers us to find kindness and connection in the precious moments of our everyday life. With rich wisdom offered through approachable takeaways and practices, this book can serve as a cherished companion you can return to again and again on the path to freedom."

—Sharon Salzberg, author of *Lovingkindness* and *Real Life*

"Susan Kaiser Greenland has improved the world immensely by bringing mindfulness to kids and parents at a time of escalating mental health challenges. Now she's taking the concept of enlightenment, often shrouded in exotica and esoterica, and bringing it into the lives of regular people in doable and fascinating ways. Bravo."

—Dan Harris, *New York Times* bestselling author of *10% Happier*

"*Real-World Enlightenment* is a beautiful book. In easily accessible, down-to-earth language, Susan Kaiser Greenland helps us appreciate that everyday glimpses of enlightenment are available right now. She shows us that it is about the small things we say and do each day. Sprinkled with compelling anecdotes and simple, easy-to-implement short practices, this book has something for everyone."

—Richard J. Davidson, *New York Times* bestselling author of *The Emotional Life of Your Brain*

"Susan Kaiser Greenland's beautifully written new book 'enlightens' us as it masterfully weaves together personal stories; Buddhist practice and teachings; literary, cultural, and philosophical references; scientific research; and practical exercises. Susan's gift, honed from years of teaching mindfulness to children, is her ability to take complex and even esoteric concepts and make them immensely relatable and accessible to us all. This book is thought-provoking, inspiring, and a joy to read."

—Diana Winston, Director of Mindfulness Education at UCLA's Mindful Awareness Research Center and author of *The Little Book of Being*

"Inspiring, clear, and practical, *Real-World Enlightenment* offers an accessible guide to seekers everywhere looking to taste the fruits of spiritual practice in everyday life. Through touching stories, scientific principles, and personal insight into timeless teachings, Susan has woven an indispensable guide to a meaningful life in these challenging, modern times."

—Oren Jay Sofer, author of *Say What You Mean* and *Your Heart Was Made for This*

"This book offers a practical way to find what many of us are seeking—waking up to a reality that's bigger than our limited self-perceptions. It draws on many spiritual traditions as well as personal stories to illustrate how enlightenment isn't some mystical state to be found only in a cave. It's a way of relating to each ordinary moment that can break us out of our usual way of seeing things and show us the beauty that's already there."

—Kristin Neff, author of *Self-Compassion*

"Every so often a book or teacher comes along that manages to be both simple and profound. In *Real-World Enlightenment*, Susan Kaiser-Greenland does just that, stripping the esoteric from the idea of enlightenment. The real world is heavy enough, and Susan Kaiser Greenland brings light and a playful energy to practice for anyone, anywhere, anytime."

—Dr. Christopher Willard, author of *Growing Up Mindful*

REAL-WORLD ENLIGHTENMENT

....

Discovering Ordinary Magic in Everyday Life

....

Susan Kaiser Greenland

SHAMBHALA

Shambhala Publications, Inc.
2129 13th Street
Boulder, Colorado 80302
www.shambhala.com

Cover art: marukopum/Shutterstock and
Lemon Workshop Design/Shutterstock
Cover design: Daniel Urban-Brown
Interior design: Greta D. Sibley

9 8 7 6 5 4 3 2 1

First Edition
Printed in the United States of America

Shambhala Publications makes every effort to print on acid-free, recycled paper.
Shambhala Publications is distributed worldwide by
Penguin Random House, Inc., and its subsidiaries.

Library of Congress Cataloging-in-Publication Data
Names: Greenland, Susan Kaiser, author.
Title: Real-world enlightenment: discovering ordinary
magic in everyday life / Susan Kaiser Greenland.
Description: Boulder: Shambhala Publications, 2024.
Identifiers: LCCN 2023033965 | ISBN 9781611809350 (trade paperback)
Subjects: LCSH: Conduct of life—Religious aspects. |
Enlightenment—Religious aspects. | Mindfulness (Psychology)—Religious aspects.
Classification: LCC BJ1595 .G755 2024 | DDC 204/.2—dc23/eng/20231206
LC record available at https://lccn.loc.gov/2023033965

To Seth, Allegra, and Gabe,
for their playfulness, attention,
balance, and compassion.

It's a little facile, maybe, and certainly hard to implement, but I'd say, as a goal in life, you could do worse than: Try to be kinder.

—George Saunders, from "Congratulations, by the Way," his 2013 convocation address at Syracuse University

CONTENTS

DISCLAIMER

Many personal stories are included in this book. All of them are true, but they are not entirely factual. I have changed where some of the stories took place, along with names, genders, and identifying characteristics of the people involved. Memory is imperfect. I recount these events to the best of my recollection.

REAL-WORLD ENLIGHTENMENT

INTRODUCTION

Golden Threads

When I started writing this book, it was not—to put it mildly—the sunniest period of my life. First, there was a global pandemic, and then I had heart surgery. On darker days, I was terrified and sad. At my worst, I felt like a phony. Who was I to write about enlightenment, given how, after meditating for decades, I am far from enlightened myself? But there were bright days too. Our grown children had returned home to sit out the pandemic, and my husband Seth and I were given a gift of family time we didn't think we'd have again. With four adults sharing workspaces, internet connections, and chores, the vibe in our household wasn't always Instagram-ready. Still, the stressful moments eventually transformed into moments of peacefulness and connection—moments of real-world enlightenment. My challenge was not to become so preoccupied by the scary stuff that I would miss them.

....

Enlightenment is a word that gets thrown
around a lot, so let's demystify it.

....

"The Tao that can be told is not the Tao" is a well-known declaration that's as true today as it was twenty-six centuries ago, when the Chinese philosopher Lao Tzu wrote his classic book *Tao Te Ching*. Like the Tao, enlightenment is what Lao Tzu and other mystics call ineffable—something that cannot be put into words. Joy is another ineffable experience: it's hard to describe, but we know how it feels. Becoming absorbed in music, dance, and creative expressions is also ineffable—indescribable but recognizable. Real-world enlightenment is like that too. It's a common experience of love and well-being that reaches far beyond us. Some call it awe, while others call it wonder. The mystics call it oneness, where we sense that everything is connected and there's no separation between the already perfect cosmos and us. Yes, the already perfect cosmos. It's a bold statement, but that's how it feels when you glimpse enlightenment. It feels like nothing is missing, that all things connect, and there's no separation between anything or anyone else and us. Sometimes the experience is intense, like a lightbulb moment, but often it's subtler. We might glimpse real-world enlightenment when we're intimate with someone or something—with nature, a loved one, an idea, or ourselves. At first, this ineffable experience is like a ring of smoke that's impossible to catch—until we sense it again, deep in the woods, reading a bedtime story to a child, sitting with a sick friend, teaching a course, meditating, praying, or resting after a hard day of work. Then, even though the idea might seem outrageous to our ordinary mindset, we have a renewed sense that enlightenment is real. We've tasted it.

Real-world enlightenment taps into an enduring, reliable sense of love, connection, and well-being that's within us regardless of our circumstances. It doesn't take much to recognize it once we know where to look, and the effort it takes has a ripple effect that benefits those around us. At first, the ripple might be small, as if we had skipped a pebble across a pond. But even little waves from tiny stones cause more ripples, that cause even more. When we swap out a large stone for the small pebble, the ripple effect grows bigger and reaches farther. It's like that when we connect with the love and well-being inside us. As our connection with them grows stronger, so does their ripple effect.

I wouldn't be surprised if you're skeptical. Enlightenment can sound like an unattainable and distant goal reserved for a select few, those who have dedicated their lives to spiritual practice and achieved a higher state of consciousness. But real-world enlightenment isn't about attaining a special status or becoming superhuman; it's about the small things we say and do every day. As we learn to look beyond our preconceived ideas and projections to see things as they truly are—made of many elements that are interdependent and changing—a sense of psychological and emotional freedom will unfold.

Still, most people who ask me about meditation are looking for something more immediate. They're juggling every imaginable type of personal and professional demand and want a toolbox of quick mindfulness-based strategies to help them manage anxiety, meltdowns, power struggles, and stress. If this sounds familiar, I wrote this guide with you in mind. Instead of focusing on a lofty goal that seems like a pipe dream, the chapters that follow encourage you to look for glimpses of enlightenment that are available right now.

A long line of teachers and teachings inspired this guide. I was raised in an interfaith home—my father was Catholic, and my mother was Presbyterian. From today's perspective, this may not seem like much of a mixed marriage, but it was a big deal in rural Michigan in the 1950s when my parents got married. My father gave up Catholicism to marry my mom, and I'm not sure he ever made peace with that decision. I was baptized, attended Sunday school, and was confirmed in the First Presbyterian Church of Paw Paw, Michigan, but still, I spent a fair amount of time in Catholic churches growing up. Almost forty years after my parents married, I followed in their footsteps into another interfaith marriage. Seth is Jewish, and I am not. Our children attended Jewish Sunday school, our daughter was a bat mitzvah, and our son was a bar mitzvah. I never converted to Judaism, nor did I rejoin a Christian church. Instead, I took a different path to study and practice Buddhism. This diverse spiritual background reinforced something I have believed for as long as I can remember. Since childhood, I saw tremendous common ground among seekers in the great wisdom lineages. This makes sense, given that Judaism, Christianity, Islam, and Buddhism, along with other religions and cultures, spread at around the same time along the "Silk Road," a network of trade routes between Europe and East Asia.[1] The more I studied and engaged in formal contemplative practice, the more convinced I became that woven through the wisdom lineages are a select group of universal themes that lead to psychological and emotional freedom. These themes are the backbone of this guide.

．．．．．．．

We have what we need to become enlightened,
but it can be hard to recognize it.

．．．．．．．

One of the most fundamental principles across wisdom traditions is that goodness is within everyone and the source of happiness. In the Mahayana, a form of Buddhism prominent in Northern Asia, goodness is also the source of enlightenment. We see people's goodness when they respond to one another with kindness, compassion, wisdom, and love. Like the sun that's always in the sky, even on a cloudy day, the innately human qualities that make up essential goodness are always with us, but sometimes they're hard to see. We can build our capacity to recognize, tap into, and embody them by understanding and internalizing the universal themes that time-honored wisdom lineages espouse. Like a restaurant that serves small plates that allow everyone to try a little of each dish, I aim to give you a taste of universal themes that offer a glimpse of enlightenment without sacrificing their complexity or nuance.

For generations, people have wondered, "How can I lead a meaningful life?" This question haunts us. It's not easily shrugged off. Whether they're scholars steeped in decades of academic study or grandparents who've learned a lifetime of lessons in the school of hard knocks, those who consider this question point to one or more time-tested, universal themes that make up a worldview that was described by a renowned sage named Padmasambhava as being as vast as the sky. I've winnowed down the list for this guide. The themes I chose are ones that have long been central to my life and work; with a nod to psychologist Jerome Bruner, I call them golden threads.[2] These golden threads weave together like fine cloth and show up repeatedly throughout the wisdom traditions. Like the shuttle traversing the warp of a loom over and over, we revisit them many times from birth until death. Our insights into the golden threads deepen with every encounter as we progress from a superficial understanding to a more nuanced one. Using repetition as a method, I return to these themes time and again throughout this guide, just as we do in daily life.

The universal themes that make up a vast, skylike view emphasize attitudes and perspectives that help us shift from a narrow survival-driven mindset to one that is both more grounded and more expansive. When we understand this broad worldview from the inside out, we become more resilient, but that's just the beginning: a view as vast as the sky charts the course for kind, resilient people to build a kinder and more resilient world. Meaningful transformation does not happen on the level of ideas alone, though; it occurs in the small actions we take every day. Padmasambhava, who was born in India during the eighth century and lived in Tibet most of his life, said this more poetically:

Though the view should be as vast as the sky,
keep your conduct as fine as barley flour.[3]

Big ideas can be changemakers only if we apply them to the small and sometimes messy things we say and do. At the end of each chapter there is a "wrap-up" section, where we consider practices and takeaways that allow us to notice the tiniest things about ourselves. That's where we will consider what it takes for our conduct to be as fine as barley flour.

I wrote *Real-World Enlightenment* for anyone interested in finding greater freedom and connection. In the decades that I have taught secular mindfulness and meditation, I've learned that pretty much everyone, regardless of their age (children and adults), is interested in exploring the nature of their minds and the world around them. If you are new to my work, welcome! If you are a parent, teacher, or caregiver who has read my other books or studied the Inner Kids model, this material will complement and enrich your work at home, at school, in the clinic, and in your community. I encourage you to dig deeper into this material by reviewing the resources referenced in the following chapters and the extensive notes at the end of this book.

This guide draws from my work, family life, and over thirty years as a Buddhist student. Learning a discipline requires serious study with serious teachers, and I am grateful to have learned from some of the best. The ideas in this book have been strongly influenced by the many teachers I've studied with over the years, especially my main teacher Yongey Mingyur Rinpoche and his brother Tsoknyi Rinpoche. (*Rinpoche* is an honorific title in the Tibetan language given to respected teachers.) I include references to their books and lectures as I describe what I learned from their profound insights into the nature of our hearts and minds.

I hope this guide will inspire you as you reach for your next transformation. Each chapter, practice, and takeaway will build upon the ones before to help you connect with the innately human qualities that lead to real-world enlightenment—a connection that grows stronger with training and practice. And there is no better arena to learn and practice them than daily life.

1

We Have What We Need to Be Free

Playfulness, Attention, Balance, and Compassion

In the chapters that follow we'll explore over thirty universal themes from time-honored wisdom lineages. Some of them, like patience and kindness, are more than big ideas; they're also essential human qualities that we can develop through training and practice. I've emphasized four of these life-changing qualities in my teaching and writing for decades.

Playfulness. There's a lighthearted, sometimes effortless, quality to playfulness that allows us to be flexible and creative, even in challenging situations. It manifests in countless ways—as a sense of humor, for instance, or as being open to new experiences without being attached to a particular outcome.

Attention. Attention allows us to be present and fully engaged. By paying close attention to our thoughts, feelings, actions, and relationships, we better understand the nature of our minds and reality. Robust and stable attention is the mental muscle we need to self-regulate. It allows us to hold off from reacting emotionally in a heated situation until we can see what's happening clearly and choose a wise response.

Balance. By finding the middle ground between extremes, balance creates a physical and emotional environment conducive to cultivating wisdom and compassion. Balance allows us to experience life with greater clarity and respond to challenges with greater equanimity and kindness.

Compassion. Compassion is the sincere desire to ease people's suffering and help them overcome challenges. It is not limited to helping those we know or people like us, but rather, compassion is a genuine wish for health and well-being that extends to everyone. Responding to pain or difficulty with patience, kindness, and understanding is an act of compassion. We offer compassion to ourselves when we recognize our own suffering, accept it as a natural part of the human experience, and respond with the same warmth and empathy that we would offer a close friend or loved one.

Playfulness, attention, balance, and compassion are not merely abstract concepts; they have real-world applications every day. We don't need to seek them outside ourselves nor reserve them for specific situations or people. They are always within us, even in challenging conditions like a particularly rough moment in Los Angeles when the city was an epicenter of the pandemic.

In November 2020, ambulances sat in hospital parking lots for hours because there weren't any open gurneys in the emergency rooms. There weren't beds in the county's intensive care units either. With the countywide surge in COVID-19 cases rising, the director of public health, Barbara Ferrer, issued a three-week "safer-at-home order." She acknowledged that public health officials were "asking a lot" when she announced that all public and private gatherings with anyone outside of a person's household were prohibited.[1]

My then almost thirty-year-old daughter had just flown to Los Angeles from New York to sit out the rest of the pandemic at our house. She was quarantining in an Airbnb for ten days before moving home and had made plans to see friends for dinner—eating outside in a socially distant way. Seth and I told her if she met with her friends, she'd need to extend her quarantine. It was early in the pandemic. The doctors hadn't learned how to treat COVID, and there were no antiviral drugs or vaccines. In our midsixties, we were in a high-risk category and weren't taking chances. We had discussed house rules related to COVID with our daughter before she decided to come home and had told her that socially distant gatherings outside with small groups of friends would be okay. A month later, life in LA had changed, and so had our house rules. My daughter was disappointed but understood. I empathized and felt conflicted, wondering if we were taking the quarantine too far. Recognizing my daughter's point of view and empathizing with her were expressions of attention and compassion.

I was working upstairs at my desk, and the law of diminishing returns had kicked in. I couldn't concentrate, so I walked down a flight of stairs to an entryway packed with stacks of partially opened cardboard boxes. We didn't shop at markets during the lockdown. Instead, we ordered everything online, from food to cleaning supplies, and had all of it delivered. There was a week's worth of half-opened deliveries in the downstairs hallway and unpacking the cardboard boxes was a big job I had been putting off. I knew from experience that focusing on a straightforward, repetitive task like this one would help me settle down. I grabbed a kitchen knife and opened the boxes one by one. I unloaded the supplies, broke down the cartons, folded them neatly, and brought the cardboard outside. I focused on making room for all of it in our too-small recycling bin. Recognizing that I felt unsettled and couldn't concentrate was a manifestation of the quality of attention. Shifting my full attention to the task at hand to settle down demonstrated balance and self-compassion.

When I returned to the hallway, Seth was there working too. Ankle deep in packing peanuts and bubble wrap, we wedged all of it into an enormous black plastic bag meant for fallen leaves. We appreciated the efficiency and accessibility of home delivery but were mortified by the waste—another example of attention and balance. We joked about how often we had packed and unpacked boxes before, reminiscing about the many times we and the kids had moved in and out of houses, dorm rooms, and apartments. Seth hoisted the jet-black leaf bag stuffed with plastic and Styrofoam over his shoulder and carried it outside. It took both of us to jam the oversized bag into the already full garbage bin. Seth hoisted me up so I could sit down on top of the leaf bag to wedge it inside, which looked as ridiculous as it sounds. When we walked back to the house to prepare dinner, we were glad to have the unpacking project behind us. Telling stories and then sitting on top of the garbage bin so the leaf bag would fit inside were expressions of playfulness.

In the kitchen making dinner, I felt a renewed appreciation for our thirty-five-plus years of householding and companionship. The unpacking project had grounded me and given me the mental bandwidth to view my daughter's quarantine through a broader lens. While working, laughing, and reminiscing with Seth, my focus had returned, and my once half-empty cup was now half-full. I'd caught a glimpse of the playfulness, attention, balance, and compassion within each of us that we can bring to any experience, even this challenging one. These four transformational qualities are always here, but unfortunately, like precious gems covered in mud, they can be hidden by the pressures of ordinary life.

Has anyone pointed out something new to you, something you think is intriguing but didn't know about before, and now that you know about it, you start to see it everywhere? You may hear about a trendy new energy drink, and then you see people drinking it all the time. Or you compliment a friend on her earrings and then see a lot of other people also wearing them. It seems like there are more of those earrings and those energy drinks than there were before, but that's not the case. It's just that you started to notice them. There's a name for this experience where something you just noticed begins to show up all the time. It's a cognitive bias called the frequency illusion or the Baader-Meinhof phenomenon.

When I first recognized playfulness, attention, balance, and compassion in everyday life, I started to see them everywhere. But something else happened that couldn't be chalked up to the Baader-Meinhof phenomenon. Unlike the energy drink or pair of earrings that we now see everywhere even though they didn't increase in number, our capacity to recognize and connect with these four essential qualities can increase. The more we tap into them, the more our ability to do so grows, like daffodils in the springtime.

In the spring and summer, hummingbirds appear out of the blue to dart in and out of our backyard. Their wings flap so quickly that all we see is a blur, but we can hear the tiny birds' wings working furiously as they hover in midair. When we stop what we're doing to watch, it feels like time stands still—until they dart away as rapidly as they came. Glimpsing playfulness, attention, balance, and compassion in daily life is a little like catching sight of a hummingbird. At first, the experience is fleeting and infrequent, but it doesn't have to stay that way.

My family loves the hummingbirds' visits, so we planted flowers to attract them. Once we had created a hummingbird-friendly garden with water to drink and places to perch, hummingbirds and their families began to show up more often and stay longer. Like building a garden that attracts hummingbirds, we can build the capacity to recognize and connect with playfulness, attention, balance, and compassion. All we need to do is create the conditions for these qualities to emerge and then cultivate them, just as we built and now tend our hummingbird garden.

WRAP-UP:
Playfulness, Attention, Balance, and Compassion

Look carefully, and you'll notice playfulness, attention, balance, and compassion are inherent within each of us. You don't need to take classes to learn about them or be an elite meditator to develop them. Like the sun in the sky that's hard to see on a cloudy afternoon, these essential human qualities are always with us, even when they are difficult to perceive. Meditation develops our capacity to see and connect with playfulness, attention, balance, and compassion more frequently and for longer periods. Mindfulness helps us bring them into daily life.

Practice

Before going to sleep, set the intention to notice playfulness, attention, balance, and compassion. If it's helpful, email or text yourself a reminder, or jot down your intention on a sticky note and post it somewhere you'll notice—the bedside table, the bathroom mirror, or the refrigerator door. The next day, look for these liberating qualities in your thoughts, emotions, conversations, actions, and reactions.

Takeaway

Consider frequency bias and whether, now that you're aware of playfulness, attention, balance, and compassion, you notice them more often. Some of these qualities will be easy to recognize, while others may be harder to see. Tapping into playfulness when you're in a challenging situation can be the toughest one to spot. Here's a pro tip: instead of looking for ways to be playful, look for ways to be effortless—ways to go with the flow.

2

Take Good Care

Safety and Kindness

A fun fact about hummingbirds is that they are wary of loud noises. Barking dogs and loud music can scare the tiny creatures away because they don't feel safe in noisy environments. People respond to unsafe environments like hummingbirds. We avoid situations that don't feel safe, and when we find ourselves in one, we don't stay long. But here's where people differ from hummingbirds: safety issues can confuse us. Sometimes, we don't recognize that the reason we're uncomfortable is because we don't feel safe, and other times we think we feel uncomfortable because we're not safe, even though that's not the reason.

What do you need to be safe and take care of yourself? The answer may not be as straightforward as it seems. Safety depends, at least in part, on whom you're with, where you are, and how you feel. When I was in my twenties and thirties, living in New York City on my own, I regularly assessed whether riding the subway at a particular hour or in a certain neighborhood was safe. Later, living in Los Angeles with young children, I made a judgment call on whether their climbing on the high bars of a rickety jungle gym was safe. When they got older, I balanced their wish to be with friends against whether their driving a long distance at night was safe. As an empty nester, my focus shifted back to Seth and me and whether choices like getting a walk-up apartment rather than one in an elevator building made sense since our ability to climb stairs carrying luggage or groceries would change as we grew older. The answers to these questions hinged on physical safety and the odds of someone getting hurt. I don't think about safety in such literal terms anymore. I now see safety as more nuanced and recognize the ways that my reactions spring from an evolutionary survival mechanism designed to keep me alive to pass my genes on to future generations, rather than critical thinking. We'll take a deeper dive into the implications of an evolutionary approach to what we do and how we feel later. For now, I encourage you to remember that we're hardwired for survival. None of the ideas or takeaways in this guide are scary. Still, some might carry you outside your comfort zone and trigger the survival mechanisms that run automatically when you're in physical danger.

When we feel safe, we're in our comfort zones, where we perform well, set appropriate boundaries, rest, recharge, and reflect. It feels good when we're in our comfort zones, but it's not where we take risks or where much growth takes place. Development takes place when we're on the far edge of our comfort zones, stretching existing skills and abilities. When a stretch is in reach, but we feel unsafe anyway, one of our innate survival mechanisms can switch into gear and shut us down. Then, a mechanism designed to protect us short-circuits our growth and gets in the way of reaching our goals. This tendency can be mitigated in several ways we'll look at later, but for now, I'll mention one: kindness. As far back as Charles Darwin, scientists, philosophers, artists, and poets have drawn a straight line between our warmhearted urge to respond to suffering with kindness and the likelihood that we'll survive, even thrive. To borrow from the preface of Dacher Keltner's excellent book, *Born to Be Good*: "[S]urvival of the kindest may be just as fitting a description of our origins as survival of the fittest."[1]

I was introduced to the poem "Kindness" from Naomi Shihab Nye's first poetry collection[2] when I heard it recited by Jon Kabat-Zinn, the founder of Mindfulness-Based Stress Reduction (MBSR). Kabat-Zinn and his teaching partner Saki Santorelli (at the time, executive director of the Center for Mindfulness at the University of Massachusetts medical school) were international rock stars in the secular mindfulness world, and I was primed to listen. It was early morning, midway through a weeklong MBSR retreat/training in the late 1990s at the Mount Madonna retreat center in Northern California. Light streamed through the floor-to-ceiling windows in the meditation hall to backlight Kabat-Zinn, who was sitting cross-legged on a meditation cushion, up on a dais. The golden early morning light gave him and the entire session an otherworldly quality. He recited the poem from memory to a room full of meditators sitting around him in a semicircle, most of whom were also sitting cross-legged on cushions. One of the images in the poem stood out then and has remained with me since:

> You must wake up with sorrow.
> You must speak to it till your voice
> catches the thread of all sorrows
> and you see the size of the cloth.

I'm struck by how often I've remembered this image of the enormity of sorrow in the world since I first heard it. The phrase has come back to me when someone I love has fallen ill or has died and when the loved ones of people close to me have struggled with illness or death. The size of the cloth hit me at an even greater level of magnitude as I watched news coverage of the Twin Towers coming down on 9/11 in New York City. The size of the cloth was almost unimaginable when I saw footage of the refrigerated trailers parked in front of hospitals in New York City functioning as temporary morgues during the early days of the pandemic. Maybe the theme of Shihab Nye's poem that "it's only kindness that makes sense anymore" resonated with me because it echoed rabbinic sage Hillel the Elder's call to action: "If not now, when? If not me, who?"[3]

Scientists have long suspected that kindness in response to other people's pain is a survival mechanism that's wired into our nervous systems. What's often harder for people to remember is that kindness in response to our own sorrow is also a survival mechanism. For many of us, being kind to ourselves is more of a leap than being kind to others. It was for me. I thought kindness was the Golden Rule we teach young children—do unto *others* as you would have them do unto you. It didn't occur to me to apply the Golden Rule to myself. I wanted to be a good mother, a good partner with Seth in providing for our family, and to make a difference in the world. I was one of the lucky ones and wanted to pay it forward. There was no room for me to take it easy. The harder I tried to do good and be good, the more of a toll it took on me. Still, it didn't register that the pace at which I was working was unkind to my family and me. I had to burn myself out emotionally and physically a few times before I could internalize the commonsense truth that discomfort is one way our bodies ask us to listen. Just as it took me a while to develop a more nuanced stance toward safety, it took me time to adopt a more expansive idea of kindness that included being kind to myself.

The practices and activity-based takeaways in this guide are designed for you to integrate into daily life easily. Doing them shouldn't be a heavy lift and tax you, but sometimes, mindfulness and meditation bring up big feelings that are painful to confront. Please be kind to yourself. Take a break if you feel overwhelmed or if discomfort becomes too much to manage easily. Time is your friend when it comes to inner discovery, and you have plenty of room to allow the process to unfold at its own pace. There's no need to rush to get something or go someplace; you already have what you need to become enlightened.

WRAP-UP: Safety

Identifying your safety needs and factoring them into your choices are a meaningful and effective way to be kind to yourself. Ask yourself, "What do I need to feel safe?" "Are my safety needs being met?" "How?" If they aren't being met, "Why not?" Remember that whether you feel safe depends on various factors, including if you're tired, hungry, or stressed. When safety and inclusion needs are unacknowledged and unmet, our nervous systems are ripe to become hijacked by one of our innate survival mechanisms.

Reflecting on safety needs can seem like a waste of time. When you're in your comfort zone, it's easy to miss the point of looking at what it takes to feel safe. Here's why you should do it anyway: If you identify your safety needs up front, while you're in your comfort zone, you can better take care of yourself later when you are outside of it. (We'll dig deeper into safety and inclusion needs in the context of interpersonal relationships later.)

Practice

Find a comfortable place where you won't be interrupted. Close your eyes or softly gaze ahead or downward. A few breaths later, listen for the loudest sound. When you are ready, listen for the quietest sound. Don't chase a sound that's hard to hear; relax and let it come to you. Let your mind be open and rest in the whole soundscape. Ask yourself, "What does it take to feel safe and welcome in a new situation?" Hold the question in mind and listen to the answers that emerge. When you're ready, open your eyes if they are closed and jot down your insights. Then, draw three concentric circles on a blank piece of paper. Prioritize your insights by writing the most important ones in the inner circle. Write those that are the least important in the outer circle. Write what's left on your list in the circle in between. All your insights matter, but double-check to ensure the essential items are in the inner circle. Review the diagram and consider ways to increase the odds that, in a new situation, you will feel safe and included. Save the diagram and put it aside. This is the first of four concentric circle drawings I'll ask you to make in this guide. We'll revisit them in the second to the last chapter, "What Matters Most."

Takeaway

How might connecting with playfulness, attention, balance, and compassion help you feel safer and more welcome?

WRAP-UP: Kindness

Throughout our evolutionary history, humans have relied on kindness to survive. Strong social bonds, effective communication, and meaningful collaboration create a supportive external environment that allows us to thrive in diverse situations and overcome challenges. Similarly, we create a supportive internal environment when we are kind to ourselves, one where we become more emotionally resilient. Kindness is a self-reinforcing behavior. By being kind to ourselves, we can better support and care for those around us. By being kind to others, we build trust, strengthen relationships, and create a sense of social support and belonging that helps us cope with stress and navigate adversity.

I first learned about the following self-compassion practice reading Zen priest Edward Espe Brown's book *No Recipe: Cooking as a Spiritual Practice* where he writes: "[I]n the early '80s, when Thich Nhat Hanh was giving a talk prior to departing from the San Francisco Zen Center where I was living, he said he had a goodbye present for us. We could, he said, open and use it anytime, and if we did not find it useful, we could simply set it aside. Then he proceeded to explain that, 'As you inhale, let your heart fill with compassion, and as you exhale, pour the compassion over your head.'"[4]

Practice

Imagine you are in a sweltering but beautiful jungle, holding a coconut shell in one hand. Can you feel the rough shell against the palm of your hand? Picture a wooden barrel filled with cool rainwater on the ground next to you. Can you see your reflection in the sparkling water? Imagine the rainwater is a nectar of compassion that soothes busy minds and big feelings. As you breathe in, imagine filling the coconut shell with compassionate rainwater. As you breathe out, imagine pouring the nectar of compassion over the crown of your head. Let go of the images of the bucket and coconut shell to focus on sensation. Imagine what it would feel like for a nectar of compassion to wash over you and soothe your body from head to toe. Starting at the crown of your head, feel the compassion rinse slowly over your face and head, then over your neck, shoulders, chest, upper arms, lower arms, and hands. Move your attention to your torso and imagine feeling a nectar of compassion wash slowly over your torso, pelvis, upper legs, knees, lower legs, and feet. When you're ready, lightly rest your attention on your outbreath. If thoughts and emotions arise, don't fight them. With no goal or purpose, allow your mind to be open and rest.

Takeaway

Find at least one way to be kind to yourself today, then see if there's a ripple effect.

3

Looking to Feel Better

Motivation and Renunciation

Why do we meditate and stay with it? Our reasons vary and change over time, but modern researchers and ancient contemplatives have come to the same conclusion: we meditate because we want to feel better. According to a 2020 research paper from Peter Sedlmeier and Jan Theumer, beginners mainly use meditation to "reduce negative aspects of life."[1] Sedlmeier and Theumer weren't the first to recognize this pattern; it dates to Siddhartha Gautama, the Buddha.

If you're familiar with Buddhist tradition, you know the story. Siddhartha Gautama was born sometime around 500 B.C.E. in Lumbini, a province in the southern foothills of the Himalayas near what is now the border between Nepal and India. Sadly, his mother died a week after he was born. His father was the leader of a small Himalayan kingdom, and Siddhartha was raised as a prince. Royal family life is an inherently sheltered environment, but Siddhartha was even more sheltered than your everyday prince. Soon after his birth, a Brahmin—a Hindu intellectual and priest—predicted that when Siddhartha grew up, he would become either a world leader who ruled a kingdom even larger than his father's or a great teacher. Siddhartha's father created a full, engaging, and protected life for the prince inside the palace walls to ensure that his son would follow in his footsteps. Hoping the prince would be content at home, he was sheltered from anything unpleasant. Siddhartha was educated and entertained, met the woman who would become his wife, married her when he came of age, and had a son, all without venturing outside the palace grounds.

Siddhartha could not contain his curiosity about the world, though. He secretly arranged with a charioteer to take him outside the palace, and for the first time, he saw people suffering from sickness, old age, and death. He arranged for a second chariot ride where he saw a wandering renunciate with serene and composed features. We don't know what Siddhartha was thinking, but something about that wandering monk and his way of being in the world was compelling. It was so compelling that Siddhartha decided to leave the comfort of his princely life to become a renunciate himself. At twenty-nine years old, he snuck out of the palace and left his belongings, family, and status behind. Siddhartha was drawn to something. Perhaps he didn't know what motivated him exactly, but he was curious about life and wanted to explore it.

In the late nineteenth century, Buddhist translators began using the English word *mindfulness* to translate *sati* in Pali or *smriti* in Sanskrit from the original Buddhist texts. Both these ancient words come from roots meaning "recollection" or "memory." As it relates to mindfulness, memory is often connected with remembering to stay with your breath while practicing mindful breathing. What we remember while mindfully investigating our inner and outer worlds is more than just attending to our breath, though. It's also remembering our motivation: why we're meditating in the first place. Just the fact that we're doing the practice reminds us of our motivation for doing it, explains Buddhist scholar and author Rupert Gethin in his essay "On Some Definitions of Mindfulness." To paraphrase:

> When they remember to pay attention to their breath, Buddhist monks also remember that they are meditating.
>
> When monks remember that they are meditating, they then remember why.
>
> When they remember they're meditating because they are a monk, they remember why they became a monk.
>
> The answer to the question, "Why did you become a monk?" is the driving force that compels a monk to meditate. It's their motivation.[2]

We don't need to be monks to be drawn to meditation. To stay with it, though, we must remember our motivation, just like monks must remember the driving force that compelled them to become monks. On the surface, my students' and my motivation to meditate are likely different from those of a monk and perhaps from each other. But deep down, the answers to the question of motivation have a common denominator whether you're a monk, a layperson, or the historical Buddha.

After leaving the palace, Siddhartha renounced all worldly goods for six years to study philosophy and meditation with the distinguished teachers of the time. As the story goes, he then joined a group of ascetics practicing meditation, eating only a grain of rice a day! At a point when he had become dangerously thin and weak, he finally accepted an offering of food from a young woman. It was a bowl of sweetened rice cooked in milk. Imagine what it must have been like to eat a bowl of rice after years of living as an ascetic. It was then that Siddhartha recognized that, to borrow a famous lyric from the rock band U2, he still hadn't found what he was looking for. Years of study and renunciation hadn't liberated him from suffering; he vowed to meditate until he achieved his goal. I imagine his now full stomach gave him the strength to sit beneath a bodhi tree and meditate for forty-nine days. There he recognized four insights into the nature of our minds and the world around us that came to be called "the four truths of the noble ones," shortened to "the four noble truths":[3]

> Suffering is an unavoidable part of life.
> It's caused by something.
> We can end it.
> There are methods to end it.

Upon recognizing those truths, he became enlightened. Siddhartha was no more; he was now the historical Buddha. He was initially reluctant to teach, but the Buddha eventually taught these four insights to a small group of disciples in a deer park in Sarnath, India.

Now we've come full circle, from the Buddha's enlightenment five centuries before the Common Era to Sedlmeier and Theumer's study in the twenty-first century. Ask any group of meditators why they practice, and you'll get lots of different answers—eighty-seven of them if you participated in one of Sedlmeier and Theumer's research studies. All eighty-seven reasons had a common denominator with each other and with the Buddha's four truths:

....

We want to be free of suffering.

....

When we talk about suffering, it's not that we suffer every minute of the day. It's more that all our experiences have at least some suffering within them. Even when we feel great joy, if we dig deeper, we're likely to be at least a little afraid of losing it.

In Buddhist teaching, freedom from suffering starts with renunciation. Not merely the external renunciation the Buddha practiced as a wandering ascetic. We'll never know how those years affected his enlightenment, but the classical story tells us that outer renunciation wasn't enough. It took a more internal renunciation for him to become enlightened. What does this mean, especially for those who aim more for real-world enlightenment than the Buddha's seemingly out-of-reach complete enlightenment? It means letting go and letting be. We let go by focusing on the goodness of what we say and do without specific expectations for the outcome. It's possible to let go of our ideas about how life should be, including some long-held beliefs about what we think will make us happy, and still work toward beneficial outcomes to make the world a better place. It's also possible to let go of our expectations for what other people will say and do while maintaining healthy personal boundaries. Big feelings bubble up when we let go of deeply entrenched expectations and beliefs, and renunciation asks us to let them be. How? By allowing them to come, go, and change. By letting go and letting be, renunciation creates an internal environment where we can be content without depending on circumstances that are outside our control.

Letting Go

We don't have to give away our possessions to let go. Money and what it can buy contribute to happiness in a meaningful way by providing security, safety, insurance, care, and an emergency cushion. Money gives us more choices about how to live our lives and a greater sense of control. But once we reach the baseline of happiness economic stability provides, more money and what it can buy contribute little to our long-term happiness. When extra material goods and worldly comforts bump up our happiness, which they sometimes do, that bump doesn't tend to last long. Modern psychology and ancient contemplative practices show that inner renunciation leads to more enduring happiness than accumulating more stuff than we need. A lovely by-product is we develop greater discernment around what to let go of and a greater appreciation of what we keep. There's wisdom in the moral of Marie Kondo's immensely popular book *The Life-Saving Magic of Tidying Up*: keep only what speaks to your heart and sparks joy.[4]

Inner renunciation is less about giving up worldly things than changing how we view and prioritize them. The starting point for adopting this perspective is recognizing and understanding what social scientists call the hedonic treadmill. We seek satisfaction by chasing after what we want and running away from what we don't want, like hamsters running on a wheel. It's relatively easy to understand that accumulating more stuff doesn't lead to lasting happiness. But what if it's not material things we're chasing after? What if we want to feel better, want someone else to be happy, don't want to be anxious, or don't want to be afraid anymore? These are legitimate desires. What's so bad about pursuing them? Absolutely nothing. Let me emphasize this point: there's nothing wrong with pursuing them. On the contrary, these are a few of the pursuits that meditation and compassion practices are designed to address. To do that, though, we need to get off the hedonic treadmill.

Mindlessly chasing after laudable desires and running away from pain yield a result that's not so different from chasing fame and fortune. We expend a ton of effort without making meaningful progress—what my late father-in-law, the New York adman Leo Greenland, used to call a lot of motion with no movement. Sure, sometimes we make some headway. But after a point, the satisfaction we gain is fleeting, so we stay on the metaphorical treadmill and keep running. We'll dig deeper into the hedonic treadmill in later chapters, but here's how it relates to our motivation to practice meditation: Deep down, we recognize that running after what we want and away from what we don't want is a vicious cycle that may make us feel good for a while, but not for long. Ultimately, the hedonic treadmill brings us no closer to the lasting contentment we seek.

Letting Be

In Tibetan, one of the main terms for renunciation—*nge jung*—can be translated as "the determination to be free."[5] "Free of what?" you might wonder. Free of the suffering that comes when we depend on circumstances outside our control to be content—like a job, another person, or a certain status. When contentment springs from our internal landscapes, our level of satisfaction increases. When it comes from circumstances outside our control, our suffering increases. The first step toward decreasing suffering is to identify its source to determine whether it's something within our control. The Buddha elaborates in the parable of the second arrow:

> When touched with a feeling of pain, the ordinary unin-structed run-of-the-mill person sorrows, grieves, and la-

ments, beats his breast, becomes distraught. So he feels two pains, physical and mental. Just as if they were to shoot a man with an arrow and, right afterward, were to shoot him with another one, so that he would feel the pains of two arrows . . .[6]

We have no control over the pain caused by the first arrow—for instance, when we get hurt in an accident, when a friend or colleague is disrespectful and mistreats us, or when someone we love is struggling and there's nothing we can do to help. The source of this pain is beyond our control. The second arrow is a different story. Suffering from the second arrow is avoidable because it is within our control.

The second arrow is not the strong, challenging emotions that emerge naturally and automatically in response to pain. Automatic reactions to pain are hardwired as part of our survival mechanisms. But if someone shot you with an arrow, would you shoot yourself with a second one? Fixating on the pain and big feelings that emerge when we're hit by the first arrow, then getting lost in a swirl of even more hurt by telling ourselves story after story about it, is like shooting ourselves with a second arrow. It escalates our suffering and extends it. That is what's avoidable. There's no second arrow if we let the pain from the first arrow alone and allow it to come, go, and change.

A friend was laid off from a job recently and given a severance package that extended her health insurance for a few months. Shortly after the job ended, she got a toothache, and when she called the dentist's office to make an appointment, she learned that her health insurance had been canceled. She was understandably furious. Her toothache, her former employer wrongfully canceling her health insurance, and her automatic emotional response were all first arrows because they were outside her control. But then came a second arrow when she called her former employer and went ballistic on the receptionist in its human resources department. My friend felt terrible when she hung up the phone. For the rest of the day, she beat herself up for having taken out her frustration on an innocent bystander. I'm not suggesting she shouldn't have called the office to solve the problem, only that by screaming at the receptionist she caused suffering that could have been avoided for both herself and someone else. Allowing emotional and psychological distress to run its course instead of acting out, or trying to get rid of it, doesn't feel good, but becoming comfortable with discomfort now is the most effective way to feel better in the long run.

Real-World Renunciation

Modern and ancient wisdom emphasize that it takes practice and commitment to let go of unhelpful beliefs and let big feelings be. Formal meditation is as good a place as any to start the process, but it's not enough. Lasting transformation comes when we remember our motivation and bring renunciation—letting go and letting be—to the small moments of each day, not just once or twice, but over and over again. Letting go of long-held beliefs and habits takes time and patience, and it can also trigger a lot of emotion. That's why renouncing small, inconsequential ones is a good place to begin.

When our family was locked down during the pandemic, Seth noticed that all of us, himself included, overused the word *interesting*—the television series one of us had just binged on Netflix was interesting; the new COVID findings were interesting; even the change in weather was interesting. He suggested that it was intellectually lazy to describe everything as interesting and challenged us to delete the word from our vocabularies. Game on. Since then, we stop ourselves from using the word *interesting*, or correct ourselves when we do, except on the rare occasion when the most thoughtful and accurate descriptor of someone or something is, well, interesting. A year or so later, my daughter learned that Seth wasn't the only one to call foul on the word. The protagonist in *Captain Fantastic* (a movie Seth had never seen) did the same thing. *Captain Fantastic* is a 2016 comedy-drama about a family living off the grid in the Pacific Northwest. The main character is a single father determined to give his six children a rigorous physical and intellectual education. Like Seth, he banned his children from using the word *interesting*. "*Interesting* is a nonword," he told his daughter after she used it to describe the provocative and disturbing novel *Lolita* by Vladimir Nabokov. "You know you're supposed to avoid it," he continued. "Be specific."[7]

The word *interesting* still slips out in our family conversations sometimes. Deeply rooted habits have a hold on us; otherwise, we wouldn't repeat them time and again. How do we motivate ourselves to work hard to change or jettison a deeply entrenched pattern and leave it behind? A scientific and philosophical principle called Occam's razor (paraphrased by the character Dwight Schrute in the hit television series *The Office* as "keep it simple, stupid"[8]) encourages us to go with the most straightforward explanation possible. To be free of suffering, we must get comfortable with discomfort. How? Through renunciation, by letting go and letting be.

WRAP-UP: Motivation

What keeps us going for the long haul? It's our motivation. Motivation is why we do what we do and why we stay with meaningful relationships and projects when the going gets rough. Given its pivotal role in our actions and relationships, one would think our motivation for doing or not doing something would be crystal clear. But that's not the case. We often have no idea what motivates us. Even when we think we know, we're often wrong.

Practice

Tune in to your body by taking a few purposeful breaths with a slight emphasis on your outbreath. When you are ready, reflect on the question, "What do I want most for myself and those I love?" Let the answers bubble up naturally, and don't try to pin them down. If nothing comes up, that's okay. Reflecting on the question is more important than answering it. Hold back from analyzing your process or analyzing the ideas that surface. Mainly, keep your attention on how you feel—on the sensory experiences beneath your analysis that add nuance to the ideas that come to mind.

When you're ready, jot down your insights and prioritize them. Then, draw three concentric circles on a piece of paper. Place your lowest priorities in the outer circle and your highest priorities in the inner circle. Place what's left in the circle between the two. Everything on your list matters, but double-check to make sure your core priorities are in the inner circle. This is the second of four concentric circle drawings I'll ask you to make in this guide. Please put it aside and save it. We'll revisit it and the similar diagrams in the chapter "What Matters Most?"

Takeaway

Every now and again, interrupt your daily routine to ask yourself, "Why am I doing what I'm doing?"

WRAP-UP: Renunciation

Renunciation isn't about giving up worldly pleasure and accepting pain; it's a shift in perspective where we let go and let be. When we see emotional and behavioral patterns for what they are—old habits that run automatically with little or nothing to do with what's happening now—we can better disentangle ourselves from the ones that aren't helpful by letting them go. When strong emotions like sadness and anger come in the wake of letting go, we let them be. The combination of letting go and letting be is renunciation. It's not nihilism, where we throw up our hands and say, "Forget it; I give up!" It's shifting our focus from a particular outcome to the process while maintaining healthy boundaries.

Practice

Choose one small, inconsequential habit you do every day and interrupt it when it starts to run. Recognizing emotional and behavioral patterns is a serious business, but this takeaway is most effective when practiced cheerfully with a sense of humor. Here are some common habits you might choose to interrupt.

Is there a word, phrase, or gesture you overuse? If so, use it in this practice.

Let go of social media if you're a habitual user. Take the apps off your phone, install an app blocker on your computer, or just stop scrolling through your feeds when you notice you're doing it.

Choose a basic activity you do several times each day with your dominant hand and do it with your nondominant hand instead. If you are right-handed, use your left hand to twist the doorknob when you open a door, for example. If you're left-handed, use your right hand to lift your morning cup of tea or mug of coffee.

Change or let go of any other small behavioral habit you do daily. For instance, my physical therapist encouraged me to stop using my hands to help me move from sitting in a chair to standing. I was floored when I saw how frequently I pushed myself up with my hands and how challenging it was to break this seemingly inconsequential habit.

Identifying the habitual patterns that drive our behavior takes a lot of thinking and reflection, but awareness of them is the essential first step.

Takeaway

How do playfulness, attention, balance, and compassion help you interrupt an inconsequential but deeply seated habit? Could you apply this insight to other aspects of your daily routine that you want to jettison or change?

4

What Seekers Seek

Yearning, Goodness, and Joy

There are those who view the amount of time I spend meditating as bizarre. Especially when my children were in elementary school and I was a practicing lawyer, friends and family wondered why I'd chip away at limited family time and vacation days to leave Seth and the kids for a couple of weeks to attend a silent meditation retreat. Their bewilderment points to the questions we'll explore in this chapter: Why do people who are successfully ensconced in the mainstream make uncommon life choices that could put their stable lifestyles at risk? What do these seekers seek?

When I took my first trip to Asia in 1988, I was a young corporate lawyer game for adventure. Seth and I were in our early thirties and had been dating for six months. We had good enough paychecks and few responsibilities, so for our first vacation together, we could have traveled pretty much anywhere and done pretty much anything. What did we choose to do? Travel to Burma (now Myanmar). Our plan? To check into the Strand Hotel in Rangoon, visit its legendary bar famous for having been frequented by the poet Rudyard Kipling and other luminaries, and once there, ask the bartender to connect us with a driver up for taking a couple of white American tourists around the country into restricted areas. This was a black-market business. The topper? Because few people in Burma wanted Burmese currency, we would pay for this adventure with three hundred one-dollar bills that Seth—after learning while in Thailand a week earlier that this travel option existed—stuffed into his underwear and smuggled through customs at the Burmese airport, past guards armed with machine guns.

I hadn't thought about our trip to Burma in many years, but it came to mind when I was writing this book. I wondered what drew sensible and responsible young professionals like Seth, me, and many others to embark on risky adventures. I remembered we wanted to take a page from the novel *The Sheltering Sky* by Paul Bowles. We yearned to be travelers, not tourists:

> Whereas the tourist generally hurries back home at the end of a few weeks or months, the traveler, belonging no more to one place than the next, moves slowly, over periods of years, from one part of the earth to another.[1]

Given our professional trajectories, becoming true travelers in our early thirties with our careers already launched was not in the cards. But we could still dream. Like travelers Kit and Port in *The Sheltering Sky* and loafer Larry Darrell in *The Razor's Edge* by Somerset Maugham (two books I read around the time we took our trip), for a month we could be slackers. "Slacker figures are fantasies of escape from a life dominated by work," writes Tom Lutz, a self-described layabout with a high-powered straight job (for many years he chaired the creative writing department at the University of California, Riverside, and is the founding editor of the *Los Angeles Review of Books*). He goes on to say in his book *Aimlessness*, "[B]ut that doesn't mean [slackers] want to stop working. Everyone loves Lebowski, but very few people want to be him."[2] What do we love about Jeff Lebowski, aka "The Dude," a character played by Jeff Bridges in the movie *The Big Lebowski*?[3] It's the ease with which he navigates his life. He doesn't get caught in the day-to-day grind. One of the things Seth and I longed for in 1988 was to step out of our usual responsibilities for a while. But there was more. We wanted to give ourselves a break, not just from work but from our egos—the relentless but often unconscious self-involved mindset that sees everything through the lens of "me." Acclaimed author George Saunders describes this perspective in his book, *A Swim in a Pond in the Rain*:

> The mind takes a vast unitary wholeness (the universe), selects one tiny segment of it (me), and starts narrating from that point of view. Just like that, that entity (George!) becomes real, and he is (surprise, surprise) located at the exact center of the universe, and everything is happening in his movie, so to speak; it is all, somehow, both for and about him.[4]

It's not that we believe that everything is happening in our own movie—the one where we're the protagonist. Intellectually, we know better. Still, without realizing it, we act like we're the center of the universe, partly because our me-oriented culture reinforces an overly self-involved mindset. Seth and I, like many who have come before and since, thought we could take a break from our achievement-oriented egos more easily if we traveled to the other side of the world. There we could connect with the vast unitary wholeness that Saunders writes about in his book—what the mystics call oneness. This wasn't a vague pipe dream. We knew what we were looking for because we'd connected with it before. Far closer to home, we had broken out of our psychological ruts to feel at one with the music we would listen to, the songs we would sing, the art we would view, and the natural world we would visit.

Listening to music, really listening, is one way I break out of my self-referential perspective to tap into a more expansive one. Whether it's a simple folk or country song, the intricate structure of a symphony, or the searching interplay of a jazz quartet, when I let myself get absorbed in music, I let go of that part of me that thinks I can control much of anything. I surrender into a sphere of direct experience where I'm sensing more than thinking. Although I grew up in a northern state, I have a thing for country music. Country music is often narrative, and I can easily get swept along by the emotions that their timeworn stories convey. Sometimes, I let go of the narrative entirely to become immersed in the rolling grooves of country music's iconic backing bands. How I feel listening to country music, though, is nothing compared to how I feel singing it. I'm no Patsy Cline, but I can carry a tune. When I'm driving in my car singing at the top of my lungs along to Steve Earle's "When I Fall" or Lucinda Williams's "Car Wheels on a Gravel Road," I am not thinking about problems, ambitions, regrets, doctors, phone calls that need to be returned, or a water bill that needs to be paid. It's as if I've taken a rocket ship outside of my mundane concerns to a mental happy place that is way less conceptual than my ordinary headspace. How I feel when I'm on my own and singing along to the radio is remarkably like how I feel chanting a mantra or how I felt as a teenager singing in the church choir. All these experiences have, at some point, been a liberating pathway out of my head and into a realm of pure joy.

Another sure path to joy for me is through nature. It has often been a literal path, the kind you hike on. Whether in the desert environment near our California home or in the eastern woods of the Hudson Valley where we used to live, getting out of the house and into nature has been a big part of my marriage. When we hike, joy often creeps up to astonish us—whether in noticing the perfect way the winter light slants through the pines on the East Coast of the United States or in spotting two red-tailed hawks gliding in an updraft below us as we walk along a canyon ridge on the West Coast. Once, while Seth and I were hiking along a densely wooded trail in Isle Royale—a national park off Michigan's Upper Peninsula—we heard rustling. We stopped, held our breath, and were treated to the sight of a massive moose not more than twenty feet away who paused to look at us before disappearing into the woods. At that moment, far from civilization and deep in the natural world, I was not thinking about myself.

Time in nature is restorative. It lifts our moods, helps our bodies rebound from stress, and aids our minds in breaking out of a mental rut so we can focus. These and other beneficial effects of nature on our mental and physical states are well documented.[5] In *The STRESS Prescription*, researcher Elissa Epel, who is cochair of the department of psychiatry at UC San Francisco, writes:

> It's simple: by shifting our physical environment, we can shift our mental state. We can change both the content of our thoughts and our thought processes. For many people, this shift is almost automatic when they place themselves

into the natural world.... It's a sanctuary environment that calms the mind and eases the body. Yes, we can train the brain to do this in our typical environment (through mindfulness practice, for example, as we discussed), but nature is a quick way to do it, and it comes with a whole host of other benefits for our mental state and nervous system.[6]

There has long been a lot of interest in what nature can provide in terms of mind-altering experiences that go beyond hiking. Writer Michael Pollan, whose career as an author and journalist has been fueled by his quest for experience, has written eight books about where the human and natural worlds intersect. His website tells us he's explored our plates, our gardens, and our minds in both the first person and the third. His blockbuster book *How to Change Your Mind* is about his two-year journey with psychedelic drugs.[7] It urges readers to seriously consider them, and a remarkable number of baby boomers in my cohort have taken Pollan at his word. Yearning to break out of their heads and their circumscribed lives, these empty nesters are experimenting with a variety of psychedelics—in their backyards, in online groups, with their therapists, and by heading to the Burning Man festival in rented RVs—with the same goal-oriented energy that fueled their high-powered careers. Some might view what they do in search of a less self-involved, more connected life as head-scratching at best and outrageous at worst, but I'm not one of them. For many people, adventurous voyages, meditation retreats, psychedelic drugs, and other immersive experiences are a modern-day hero's journey.

The hero's journey is an archetypal story fueled by yearning that follows a familiar pattern. Someone leaves their conventional life behind because they're searching for something—a spiritual experience, an understanding, an adventure. On this journey, they navigate an unfamiliar and dangerous world. When they find what they're looking for, they are transformed. The hero's journey is a well-trod romantic arc explored by both academic Joseph Campbell and filmmaker George Lucas. In archetypal stories that follow this model, the hero returns to their ordinary life and uses what they learned to help others. When embarking on a real-life hero's journey, though, what seekers often overlook is that the hero's journey doesn't necessarily end well. It didn't for the two main characters in *The Sheltering Sky,* Port and Kit—one died, and the other went mad. Nor did it go well for three rabbis in *As a Driven Leaf,* by Milton Steinberg, a historical novel set in Roman Palestine in the first half of the second century, the most powerful and upsetting hero's journey I've read. Steinberg's story tells of three Talmudic rabbis whose search for meaning led one to death, another to madness, and the third—Elisha, the protagonist—to excommunication.[8] It's unfortunate, but true, that transformation doesn't always have a happy ending.

So why risk it?

The root of the word *yearn* is the Old English word *giernan,* which means "to strive, to be eager, desire, seek for, beg, or demand."[9] Yearning is emotional; it feels like something is missing and there's a melancholy associated with it. Unlike the desire that fuels the hedonic treadmill, fixated as it is on getting something or somewhere, the bittersweet longing that fuels our search for meaning is not fixated on getting something or someplace. It's fueled by tenderness and compassion, like the homesickness of a mother bird who's away from her nest. She yearns to get home because that's where she left her baby birds. Like a mother bird flying back to her nest, we know that joy and contentment are within reach because we've been there before. How do we connect with them again? In his book *Turning Confusion into Clarity*, Mingyur Rinpoche tells a story about feeling homesick when he was a young monk living in a monastery. His retreat teacher Saljay Rinpoche reassured him that everyone gets homesick when they long for comfort outside themselves.[10]

....

Our true home is inside us.

....

Perhaps the most fundamental tenet in Buddhist thought is that lasting joy and contentment can't be found outside ourselves. We're born with the essence of what we seek. As corny as it might sound, there are seedlings of goodness inside us. This garden of goodness feels like a home base, a refuge, or a port in the storm. Like seedlings, our connection to goodness grows when we nurture it. We can rest in our goodness more easily when we recognize and develop the essential human qualities that resonate within us, like playfulness, attention, balance, and compassion. Why? Because they lead us away from "the usual messy aimless impulse-driven way of life" that novelist and playwright Christopher Isherwood described in *My Guru and His Disciple*, another book about seekers and what they seek that I read around the time of our first trip to Asia.[11] If these transformative qualities lead us away from an ego-driven life, where do they take us? Remembering Occam's razor, there's a simple answer that dates to the historical Buddha: qualities like playfulness, attention, balance, and compassion tap into our inherent goodness, and the essence of goodness is joy.

The Hubble Space Telescope has changed our understanding of the universe and our place in it. Since its launch in 1990, Hubble has sent us over a million detailed observations that reach far out in space and back in time. It's helped scientists discover black holes, dark matter, and newly forming planetary systems. On Christmas 2021, the James Webb Space Telescope joined Hubble in space. Larger and more advanced, Webb can reach back 13.5 billion years to see the early universe and watch the formation of the first stars and galaxies.[12] The perspectives of these two magnificent telescopes are so vast that it's hard to imagine. When we compare them with our own, the limitation of human perception becomes crystal clear—so much so that it's hard to feel anything but intellectual humility in response.

I find it helpful to remind myself of this when I sense something's missing that I can't pin down; when I'm yearning for something, but don't know what it is. Perhaps singer-songwriter and poet Leonard Cohen best captured the ineffable characteristic of yearning when, in two interviews included in the documentary *Hallelujah: Leonard Cohen, a Journey, a Song,* Cohen was asked about the depressive episodes he suffered in his youth. In the first, he answered,

> They've lifted, they've lifted completely. It's not so much that I got what I was looking for but the search itself dissolved.

In a second clip from the same documentary, another interviewer said, "It sounds like you had an amazing moment of clarity or revelation or whatever." Cohen disagreed:

> It wasn't as dramatic as that, I mean there were no bright lights, but something did happen, and God knows I want to celebrate it . . .

He continued,

> But I certainly know that any analysis of it would be futile.[13]

In these interviews, Cohen embodies intellectual humility.

Like those aspects of space and time that we can't see but can be detected by the Hubble or Webb telescopes, there are aspects of life that are futile to analyze because they're beyond our human perspective. In these interviews, Cohen lets us know that he's become comfortable with the conceptual limitations of being human and the uncertainty that comes with them. No bright lights, nothing dramatic, but surely cause for celebration.

Seth and I have traveled to Asia several times since that first trip in 1988, both for work and pleasure. Our perspectives broadened with each visit as we met new people, navigated different cultures, and saw things we hadn't before. But never again did yearning fuel one of our adventures like it fueled our Burma trip. Nor did we again experience the vivid newness and sheer unadulterated joy that came with the thrill of driving from Rangoon (now Yangon) to the Temples of Pagan (now Bagan) in the open back of a dilapidated Jeep. Maybe that experience was extreme because we were young and so was our relationship. Or maybe our joyful experiences since have been subtler because both of us have found much of what we're looking for. Regardless, the trip to Burma was pivotal for me. It gave me a taste of real-world enlightenment and the motivation to do whatever it would take to bring it home with me.

WRAP-UP: Yearning, Goodness, and Joy

Since the beginning of time, humans have yearned to break free of the limitations of our narrow, ego-driven perspectives to connect with the vast unitary universe of which we are just a tiny part. It's a relief when we are not fixated on viewing life through the lens of I, me, and mine. By dropping our egos, we free up intellectual and emotional resources to recognize and connect with the goodness within and around us. There's another upside, too: joy. Joy is a natural result of dropping ego and recognizing goodness. Art, music, and nature are three well-trod pathways to letting go of ego, connecting to goodness, and experiencing joy. In the next two practices, we'll surrender to music and nature. Both ground us and help put things in perspective.

Music

Scientists from UC Berkeley have found that music evokes at least thirteen(!) emotions: amusement, joy, eroticism, beauty, relaxation, sadness, dreaminess, triumph, anxiety, scariness, annoyance, defiance, and feeling pumped up.[14] When we're absorbed in music and the emotions it evokes, it's easier to let go of a narrow, ego-driven mindset and connect with a more expansive one.

Practice 1

Choose a song that resonates with you, then find a comfortable place where you won't be interrupted. Make sure you have room to move. Take time to settle, then play the song and close your eyes. Allow yourself to become absorbed in the music. Dance if you want to dance, sing if you want to sing, and be still if that's what you want to do. It's natural if your mind wanders; just bring it back to the music. When thoughts and emotions bubble up, let them be. Relax into the song's energy and surrender to the emotions it evokes.

Nature

In the 1980s, doctors in Japan developed a medicinal practice called *shinrin-yoku*. Translated, it means "forest bathing," and the Japanese were all in. Forest bathing gave people a breather from their hectic lives and an opportunity to forge a bond with Japan's breathtaking forests. By the 1990s, forest bathing had become so popular in Japan that scientists got curious and began to study it. Researchers found that our age-old inclination to seek solace outdoors is genuinely therapeutic and that there's a physiological upside to immersing ourselves in nature. Japanese studies showed that forest bathing improves sleep, mood, and focus while lowering stress levels. If you think forest bathing is a hardcore wilderness retreat, think again. Forest bathing can be as accessible as soaking in your natural surroundings while you stroll in a local park.

Practice 2

Take a break from what you're doing and go outside. Find a spot where you can sit, walk, or lie down. Ideally, the place is green (near trees and other plants), blue (near water, an ocean, river, lake, or waterfall), or both. Don't worry if a less colorful cityscape is your best option. There's tremendous value in simply getting outside plus plenty of sensory information to take in wherever you are.

To practice, get comfortable and then, without trying to change anything, bring awareness to your posture. If you're walking, bring awareness to your gait and how you carry yourself. If seated or lying down, bring awareness to how you hold yourself. If you want to adjust your gait or posture now that you've become aware of it, go ahead and do so. Now, soak up what's coming in through your senses—the sounds, the breezes, the sunlight, and the smells. Notice the goodness that's in and around you. Take in the feeling of being connected to something bigger than yourself.

Takeaway

Enjoy the positive vibes and sensory pleasures of listening to music and spending time in nature. Appreciate the goodness that you see, hear, and feel. Drink it up!

5

For Everyone and Everything

Humility and Its Ripple Effect

The best shorthand insight into intellectual humility I've read was in a tweet from organizational psychologist Adam Grant: "Wisdom often ends in a question mark, not an exclamation point."[1] Since our hardwiring and life experiences limit our perception, aspects of every experience are outside our awareness. No matter how closely we look at what's happening, it's impossible to know all the causes and conditions that led up to this very moment. Everything we think or believe is an educated guess. When we closely watch what's happening in our internal and external worlds, we see that everything is made up of countless connected elements that move, change, and commingle. Internalizing this understanding of three universal themes that we'll dig deeper into later—interdependence, impermanence, and multiplicity—is an example of intellectual humility that is often hard-earned. It's well worth the effort, though. Humility creates the space for a more nuanced understanding of absolutely everything to emerge, including how best to take care of ourselves and others.

In the same way that charity begins at home, meditation starts with a focus on us. If, like so many of us, you identify with being a caregiver, it's helpful to remember that when you take care of yourself, you are also caring for other people. It's a lesson that is easy to forget. The renunciation we explored in "Looking to Feel Better" and the yearning we considered in "What Seekers Seek" can seem solely centered on our internal experience. That's why it's common for me to hear some version of this: "Meditation is okay for stress reduction and emotional healing. After that, it seems self-involved, verging on narcissistic. Why spend so much time meditating on my own when I could be working or connecting with family and friends?" It's a good question and one that classical meditation texts answer. In Mahayana Buddhism, which teaches that everyone—not just the historical Buddha, but everyone—has the potential for awakening, people meditate to fulfill a gigantic aspiration. The aspiration is to end suffering entirely—not just our suffering, not just someone else's, but everyone's. Especially in a chapter where one of the themes is humility, isn't it presumptuous to aspire to end someone else's suffering, much less everyone's? Only if we assume we know what's best for other people.

....

We embody intellectual humility when we focus
on what we say and do, instead of the outcome.

....

Suppose you're like most of us and initially look to meditation for stress reduction and emotional healing. It makes sense to hope these practices will make you feel better. Dig a little deeper, though, and I bet you also hope meditation will help someone else—your coworkers, your children maybe, or your partner. I'll take this one step further and wager that if you are better able to handle stress since you took up meditation—if you're even a little less reactive or anxious—you're already helping other people with your practice. Follow that thread, and I bet your meditation is helpful beyond your circle of close friends and family. If your coworker tries the meditation app you suggested, your practice is already having a ripple effect. When you see the beneficial ripple effect that comes from focusing on the process (your meditation practice) rather than the outcome (feeling calm, for instance, or a decrease in excess stress), the gigantic aspiration from the Mahayana tradition to help all beings without exception becomes less far-fetched. Of course, it is presumptuous to think that we have the power to help all beings, but the very aspiration to do so opens our hearts and means that we don't exclude anyone from the scope of our caring and connection.

When we learn more about our minds, hearts, and bodies, we begin a robust process of inner transformation, which naturally leads to outer transformation where renunciation and compassion are linked like the two wings a bird needs to fly. "Compassion and true renunciation are very similar; the difference is the focus of the contemplation," writes the Dalai Lama in his book *The Middle Way: Faith Grounded in Reason.* "[T]rue renunciation relates to ourselves and our own suffering, while compassion relates to other sentient beings and their suffering."[2] At the most basic level, when we let go of old behavioral and emotional habits that have been getting in our way, we start to feel better. That's renunciation. When we feel better, we have the mental bandwidth to recognize what matters. That's love and compassion. Practicing renunciation, love, and compassion is how we focus what we say and do on goodness, not outcome. There will still be a result, though, even when we don't focus on it. Often, the outcome is that we are more available to connect with other people. Meaningful connections make us feel better. When we feel better, we're easier to be around, and that's another example of the ripple effect of our practice!

Don't be surprised when you start seeing this ripple effect grow. I have worked in many schools, and countless times I've seen what happens when just one teacher, in just one classroom, integrates mindfulness into their routine. Parents, administrators, and faculty members ask, "What's happening in this classroom? Something feels different." Soon, other teachers ask how to bring mindfulness into their classrooms, even those who were resistant initially. As more classrooms become mindful, the benefits ripple out further at school and in the homes of teachers and students. Something similar happens in community-based family programs. When one family starts to practice, other parents take notice. Then, mindfulness and meditation no longer seem far-fetched and distant to families who hadn't experienced them before, and those families are more inclined to practice too.

The motivation to end suffering entirely is acknowledged explicitly in many classical training methods. At the start of each session, meditators offer an aspiration to remind themselves that they hope their practice will help others. Then, at the end of each session, meditators offer a dedication where they voice their hope that the practice they just completed benefits others. The aspiration at the beginning and the dedication at the end of each meditation session can be said silently or aloud. It might be as formal as a prayer in a foreign language or as simple as the one I silently say to myself before and after I teach: "May this be helpful." All that matters is that meditators hold in mind the bigger purpose of their practice, which, at heart, is one of connection.

In an interview on Ezra Klein's podcast, megasuccessful

record producer Rick Rubin described a more elaborate ritual of connection than the one I practice before I teach. It was something he envisioned before recording the podcast with Klein:

> I did a ritual for us where I imagined my higher self—I envisioned my higher self floating above me.
>
> And I envisioned you [Ezra Klein, the podcaster] and I envisioned your higher self floating above you. And then, my higher self and your higher self embraced and agreed that we would work together to bring forth the best information that would be helpful to others.
>
> Now, you didn't know about that when we started, but that was something I did for myself with the idea of that's the outcome that I'm hoping for. And that little ritual probably had some impact on me. It may have had an impact on you. I can't say. I don't know. But I know that it's like setting an intention.
>
> When you set an intention, like belief, it has power. So I come in feeling—I come into this conversation with a sense of connection with you, an imaginary sense of connection with you, in the hopes that that'll be beneficial to what we're doing together today. That's one example of a ritual.[3]

The wish to help all beings might sound like a big responsibility that's too much to take on. But Rubin's ritual illustrates that just imagining a connection with someone may positively affect them. Holding in mind an altruistic motivation isn't the same as taking on other people's problems, nor does it tax you the way you might think it would. Remember Occam's razor, the scientific and philosophical principle that encourages us to keep things simple? All it takes to set an altruistic motivation is to fuel your meditation with the hope that it's helpful—in your aspiration at the beginning, your practice in the middle, and your dedication at the end. It works because it's so simple.

The simplest approach is often the fastest route to understanding why we do what we do outside of meditation, too. Sometimes, we react the way we do because one of our survival mechanisms has bypassed our thinking mind entirely and our nervous system is running the show. If I had known more about this dynamic as a young professional, mom, and wife, life would have been easier for my family and me. I hadn't internalized then why it's hard for people to think clearly when they're having a meltdown. Nor why it's hard to reason with someone who has lost their cool. Nor that people are more likely to have a short fuse when they're tired, hungry, stressed, or all three. In the next chapter, we will consider some of our inborn survival mechanisms and reflect on how they affect learning and growth.

WRAP-UP: Humility and Its Ripple Effect

Our brains predict what someone wants and how someone feels based on our life experiences. Predictions are far from a certainty, though. Even with the best intentions, what we think will help others is guesswork. Do we throw up our hands and say, "Why bother?" Nope. We keep our sense of humor and welcome a humbler perspective. Intellectual humility can have consequences that reach far beyond our immediate surroundings.

For every action there's a corresponding reaction—one thing leads to another and another. Knowing this, we see that what we say and do affects other people and things. Even small actions and inactions can launch a ripple effect that leads to significant outcomes. Some of those outcomes are helpful, but others are not. Just ask my grown children. I can easily underestimate the vast discrepancies between my past experiences and their current ones. Given that I write and teach about intellectual humility, it shouldn't surprise me when the advice I give them isn't helpful. Still, it can be challenging to zip my lip. I aspire to ask more questions instead of shutting down entirely and to focus on the process instead of the result.

Practice

Hold back from offering unsolicited advice. Instead, work to develop intellectual humility by reflecting on what you would have said had you voiced your opinion. How certain are you that you would have been correct? Tune in to your body for clues. What didn't you know that might have changed your mind?

Takeaway

If you're tempted to offer unsolicited advice, ask questions instead. Then, see if there's a beneficial ripple effect.

6

Survival 2.0

Relaxation and Love

Tell me to relax, and my jaw will clench. It's like hearing finger-nails scratch across a chalkboard. Still, I open this chapter by encouraging you to relax, no matter what. Why? Because relaxing in the face of physical and emotional discomfort is a game changer.

Survival is our evolutionary imperative, so we're hardwired to pay attention to what scares us. Reproduction isn't everyone's intention, but still, survival of the human species is built into everyone's nervous system. When we're frightened, our brains orchestrate an elegant physiological response designed to fend off physical threats by releasing a flood of chemicals in the form of hormones like cortisol and adrenaline. "When the fight-or-flight system fires, every system in our body is changed," says Shannon Bennett, PhD, clinical director for New York Presbyterian Hospital's Youth Anxiety Center, in an interview with Verywell Health.[1] Our hearts beat faster to pump blood into our large muscles to prepare to flee; our pupils dilate to focus on the threat; our digestion slows so that urgent bodily functions will be able to perform optimally; and our muscles tense to fight. Taut muscles protect us like a suit of armor and guard against physical injury.

This doesn't feel good, and it's not supposed to because our top priority is to survive an immediate physical threat. But here's the problem: Our stress response can get triggered when we're not in physical danger—when we're worried about meeting a deadline for a project, for example, or arguing with our best friend. It can commandeer so much energy that we lack the stamina and mental bandwidth to think through a problem carefully. With our capacity to think strategically reduced, we are more likely to react impulsively to a situation than respond thoughtfully.

One way to work with the stress response is to become aware of our big emotions and sensations, as well as the thoughts that fuel them, and then shift our attention to a neutral or pleasant object and focus on it. The object of our attention is called an anchor, and it functions like an anchor for a ship. As a ship's anchor keeps a boat from drifting out to sea, a meditation anchor keeps our attention focused on the present. The way we pay attention to a meditation anchor is like how we pay attention when driving a car; we focus on the road primarily, but we also keep an eye on street signs, what's in our rearview mirror, and what's playing on the radio. Anchor practices in meditation are similar. We don't aim to eliminate distractions—the thoughts, feelings, other noises, or physical sensations that bubble up when we meditate. We aim to notice them without getting swept away by them. It's natural to get distracted sometimes, and when that happens, we gently return our attention to our anchor without blocking the distracting thoughts, emotions, or sensations. Then, our nervous systems can ease back into balance. Focusing on an anchor during meditation or daily life is one way to hone the concentration it takes to steady ourselves. Once we're emotionally regulated and mentally responsive, we can choose from various resources—calling a good friend, going for a walk, or seeking professional support, for instance—to help us better navigate what is challenging us.

Anchor practices sound simple enough, but they're not always easy. They require robust, stable attention, a commodity that's in short supply when we're stressed and feel tense. Anchor practices are most helpful when we relax, but sometimes our bodies refuse to cooperate. It's tough to relax when one of our brain's protective mechanisms has kicked into gear, even if we know from experience that we think more clearly and feel better when we do. Luckily, there are other options. One of them is to draw upon a different hardwired protective mechanism: kindness and human connection. If we're wound up and unable to relax, we can switch gears to meet what's happening with love.

Folk music fans will remember "Love Is Just a Four-Letter Word," a song written by Bob Dylan but never recorded or performed by him. It only became popular when Joan Baez recorded and performed it. Whether their ill-fated romance influenced Baez's choice to sing the song and Dylan's choice not to sing it is a mystery. It's reasonable to assume, though, that love was a loaded word for them. ("Love's a Loaded Word" is the title of another popular song from the 1960s; this one from the American rock band The Byrds.)[2] If love is a loaded word for you too, please stay with me.

Romantic love has been a central theme in art since the beginning. In popular music, there have always been megahits about love and passion. Through the ages, literature and romantic comedies, or "rom-coms," have also exalted amorous love. In *The Iliad*, the character Hera (Goddess of the Sky and wife/sister of Zeus) hatches a plot to distract her husband from a pivotal battle in the Trojan War by seducing him. This well-known passage from Homer's epic poem is from Hera's soliloquy: "There is the heat of love, the pulsing rush of longing, the lover's whisper, irresistible—magic to make the sanest man go mad."[3]

Literature's expansive format lends itself to looking beyond romantic love to a view of love that doesn't need another person as its object—one that doesn't need an object at all. In Leo Tolstoy's classic novel *War and Peace*, Prince Andrei's insight after having been wounded on the battlefield was that the noble love he first experienced while dying—when he saw his enemy yet still loved him—"is the very essence of the soul and needs no object."[4] Alan Watts's landmark book of spiritual discovery, *The Wisdom of Insecurity*, points to agendaless love as central to the human experience. Watts goes so far as to call this love the "organizing and unifying principle" that creates community.

> For the love that expresses itself in creative action is something much more than an emotion. It is not something which you can "feel" and "know," remember and define. Love is the organizing and unifying principle which makes the world a universe and the disintegrated mass a community. It is the very essence and character of mind, and becomes manifest in action when the mind is whole.[5]

The agendaless love that's an organizing and unifying principle and the very essence of the soul is not squishy nor New Age. It is our birthright. This type of love doesn't feel enchanted like the high-flying love of romantic songs, novels, and rom-coms; it feels familiar, grounded, and down-to-earth. It's a sense of warmth and care so deeply wired into our minds and hearts that it's easy to miss. In romantic movies, love is accompanied by fireworks and swells of sentimental music. Sometimes people expect all types of love to feel like that dreamy, silver-screen experience. But the noble love that's an organizing and unifying principle feels less like the climactic moment in a rom-com and more like a homecoming. When we connect with it, we feel safe and content. It's like finding our way back home.

Heart surgery is a challenging experience under the best of circumstances, and it was tough during the height of the COVID pandemic. In many hospitals, patients had to go it alone. My surgery was scheduled for when the first Omicron wave of the pandemic was at its peak. Infections had skyrocketed, and no visitors were allowed. Seth drove me to the hospital on the morning of my surgery and dropped me off at 5 a.m. The look on his face when we said goodbye at the waiting room door reminded me of how I felt when we dropped off our kids at college orientation and, before that, the first time we dropped them off at summer camp. Even though I knew better, it felt like I might never see them again. On the morning of my surgery, I was the child being dropped off at summer camp; I felt it could be the last time I'd see Seth. The adult me figured I'd be okay, but deep down, I was frightened by the remote chance that something would go terribly wrong.

A surgical aide closed the waiting room door and walked another heart patient and me down a dark, windowless hallway to the room where we would be prepped for surgery. My companion was a father with two young children who had said goodbye to his wife in the hospital parking lot. At sixty-five, I thought I was young for heart surgery, but he was much younger. On the long walk down a short hallway, he told me it was his second heart operation; his first one hadn't worked. He was looking at longer odds of success and a longer recovery time than I was. Both of us were nervous. When we got to the prep room, we wished each other luck as the clinician gave us gowns to change into and plastic bags for our belongings. She pulled one curtain around his gurney and another around mine. I expected we'd meet again in the Cardiac Intensive Care Unit the next day, but I never did see him. I hope he's okay.

As soon as I had changed, a sea of busy strangers bustled around me. They gave me an ID bracelet, took my valuables, asked questions, and prepared me for surgery. Or, more accurately, they tried to prepare me for surgery. As much as I knew intellectually that the clinicians were well-trained and there to help, my body tensed up like a metal suit of armor. Weirdly, I had no idea I was tense until the clinician told me so. I must have left my critical thinking and perspective in the waiting room with Seth because I thought I was being a model patient.

My hallway companion and I weren't the only ones who felt stressed that morning. The young clinician from the anesthesiology department who was prepping me was under pressure, too. On the other side of the thin curtain the nurse had pulled around my gurney to separate us from everyone else, people were urging him to hurry so they could get me to the operating room on time. He was racing against the clock and had difficulty finding a vein. My body was not cooperating. I wish I could tell you that my meditation practice kicked in at that moment, that I relaxed my mind and my body relaxed in response. But my being an ideal, mindful patient was not in the cards. I was scared, and my intellect had stopped running the show; my nervous system had taken over. This was not a positive development for the clinician or me. My intellect needed to be more emotionally intelligent, and my emotions needed to be more insightful.

Like an angel, one of the surgeons appeared at the side of my gurney and started a conversation with us. Given her easygoing tone and manner, you'd think we were old friends who had run into each other at the supermarket. She talked to me about her work and mine. She held my hand with one hand and passed the clinician a tool he needed with her other hand. The clinician remarked on how unusual it was for a surgeon to pitch in and help. She smiled and told him she had trained at the county hospital, where everyone helped each other. The mood in the room shifted. The clinician found a vein, the IV was in my arm, and I was going to surgery. Luckily for the clinician and me, the surgeon had lent us her nervous system that morning; she recognized that we were struggling and met us with care and connection.

Meeting experience with love doesn't mean condoning bad behavior or letting go of a skillful response. It only asks that we approach the experience with the intention to love. When we're open to the full range of our emotions, we can touch an immense sense of love even in the most challenging situations. When we do, it becomes possible to negotiate whatever we face with playfulness, attention, balance, and compassion.

The warmth and care the surgeon brought to work that morning embodied the highest form of love. This love is noble, tender, open, and expects nothing in return. Agendaless love lightens our loads and brings us together. You may think you're alone and there's no one like this surgeon you can connect with, but purposeless love is everywhere. Walk in the park or sit on a park bench and watch the passersby. At first, people may seem guarded and self-involved, but flash them a smile, and barriers will drop. Some people will smile back at you, others will say hello, and a dog might run over to you wagging its tail and looking to be petted. Suddenly, the world seems like a friendlier place—warmer and more connected.

When our nervous systems are on high alert, it's tough to be open to expressions of love and even harder to reach out and love someone. When we are guarded, how do we connect with noble love, a core element of our natural goodness and fundamental sense of well-being? We relax. Relaxation is in a feedback loop with love; when relaxation feels out of reach, love will help us relax. When love feels out of reach, relaxation will help us connect with it. Both are contagious.

On the morning of my surgery, I was lucky there was someone there to meet me with love. But even when we're on our own, there's noble love to tap into. Being loving toward yourself can be harder than expressing love to someone else, but anyone can do it if you know what to look for and where to look. One straightforward way to understand how to look is by reframing the Golden Rule. Instead of "Do unto others as you would like others to do unto you," practice "caring for yourself as well as you care for others." If you value honesty, be at least as honest with yourself as you are with friends and family. If you let people off the hook for their mistakes and imperfections, be at least as forgiving with yourself as you are with them. If you are patient with others, be patient with yourself too. Telling yourself to be honest, forgiving, loving, and patient can backfire, though, the same way someone telling me to relax can backfire. Just thinking about developing these laudable qualities when we don't feel them can seem like pressure and put us on edge. Centuries-old meditation practices offer an effective solution to this conundrum by harnessing the power of imagination.

Imagination practice in meditation is called *visualization*, a term that can sound esoteric but doesn't need to be. We visualize all the time—it is an essential part of thinking—and when we do, we engage our entire central nervous system, our total being. What we see in our imaginations also informs what we hear, taste, smell, touch, and feel. In her book, *The Extended Mind: The Power of Thinking outside the Brain*, Annie Murphy Paul writes, "Humans solve problems most effectively by imagining themselves into a given scenario."[6] We practice visualization every day: chicken or fish for dinner tonight, or what about takeout? We hold each meal in mind, however briefly, and choose the most appealing one. Where should we go on vacation? Head to a warm weather destination for winter break or a snowy one? We imagine each scenario and decide where we'd most like to go.

Just as imagination is essential for planning and organizing daily life, imagination practices are important in meditation training, especially in Vajrayana Buddhism, which is mainly practiced in the Tibetan tradition. Since anything can happen in our imaginations, visualization practices open the door to a limitless range of experiences, some that we know and others we can only imagine. When we talk about visualizing, "we are simply talking about the human habit of imagination, which we rely on to help negotiate all our activities," writes Mingyur Rinpoche in his book *Turning Confusion into Clarity*.[7] He explains that this same "human habit" can be applied to the meditation method we call visualization. Even an irritable and cranky person can visualize themselves as patient, honest, open, forgiving, and loving. In our imaginations, even the most uptight person among us can relax. All we need to do is couple playfulness with the power of attention like Rick Rubin did in the story I told earlier, when he set a positive intention for the outcome of a podcast by imagining himself and the interviewer Ezra Klein hugging each other before they recorded the session.

WRAP-UP: Relaxation

For many of us, our knee-jerk reaction to stress is trying to think through our problems, even when doing so is not helpful. The noise in our head escalates, and our body tightens in response. While it might sound counterintuitive, when we're upset it's a more effective grounding strategy to move our attention away from what's happening in our minds to the sensations in our bodies. This simple shift in our awareness helps us to relax.

Practice

Slowly scan your body from the crown of your head to the tips of your toes. Start by imagining what it would feel like to pull a soft, knit beanie over the crown of your head. Feel the cap's soft, snug fit against the top of your head and your forehead, then against the back and the sides of your head. Imagine how it feels to pull the beanie down over your ears. Now, shift your gentle, curious attention to your face and feel the muscles around your eyes, then feel your cheeks, jaw, then neck. Slowly move your attention from your neck to feel your shoulders, upper arms, lower arms, hands, then fingers. Feel your chest, belly, then rear. Continue moving your attention down your body slowly to feel your upper legs, knees, lower legs, feet, then toes. Notice how your body feels when you pay attention to it. Do the sensations change when you become aware of them? Does space open in your heart and mind? Do you feel more relaxed?

Takeaway

When you feel upset or stressed, shift your attention from thoughts to physical sensations. Feel your feet on the ground, the breath in your belly, or the sensations in your hands. Can you soften and relax?

WRAP-UP: Love

People are hardwired for love. Whether it's a high-flying passion like a new romance or a quiet and tender devotion like a parent's bond with their child, love is a profound connection that brings people together. Love is boundless and always present. We don't need to love someone or something to experience love because it doesn't require an object. This can be hard to grasp intellectually, but we get closer to understanding the boundless nature of love when we harness the power of our imaginations.

Practice

Reflect on someone or something you love dearly. Maybe it's a pet, family member, or close friend. Maybe it's romantic love that you choose to remember. Close your eyes and get comfortable. Lightly place your attention on the outbreath as you breathe naturally. When you're ready, imagine you're with the one you love. They're smiling at you (or wagging their tail, or cuddling), and you're happy to be with them. Without thinking about it too much, imagine letting the person you're holding in mind know that you love them. You could imagine hugging them, for example, or saying, "I love you." Pay close attention to the thoughts, emotions, and sensations that come up without analyzing them. If they feel good, soak them in. Notice difficult thoughts, feelings, or sensations that bubble up without engaging with them, or if nothing comes up at all, imagine how you'd like to feel when you express love and picture that.

Now, bring to mind an image of yourself—picture yourself as a child, as you are now, or at any point in time and space, real or pretend. Imagine that the you in the picture is alive and well. Silently let the mental image of yourself know that you love them. Take in the feeling of being loved without getting caught in your emotions. Notice if you don't feel anything, or if difficult feelings bubble up. Then picture what it would be like to choose to love yourself. How would you like love to feel? Imagine feeling that way. When you're ready, let go of the visualization to rest in open awareness.

Takeaway

With friends, family, lovers, pets, and on your own, feel the love. Drink up the love within and around you for as long and as often as possible.

7

Don't Think about a White Bear

Allowing, Appreciation, and Self-Compassion

A common knee-jerk reaction to tough situations and big feelings is to bear down and muscle through. I used to do that. Another common reaction is to ignore them. Both approaches get something wrong. They assume the conscious, problem-solving mind is running the show like the chief executive officer of a corporation.[1] Operationally, the problem-solving mind is the "me" that thinks through issues and puzzles them out, so it makes sense we identify with it. It seems to make the decisions that direct what we say, what we do, and how we feel. In truth, the problem-solving mind works in partnership with a broader more all-encompassing mind that's busy in the background gathering information about what's happening inside and out, always with the deeper evolutionary motive to keep us safe to reproduce. It's this broader mind working in the background that directs our energy. When it senses danger, it shifts resources away from the frontal lobe where we solve problems to the basic tasks of survival. In extreme cases, our problem-solving minds either freeze like the spinning rainbow-colored beach ball on a locked-up Apple computer screen (or the dreaded "blue screen of death" on a Windows computer) or start a stream of worrisome thoughts and emotions that gain momentum like a snowball rolling downhill (called a negative spiral), making critical thinking difficult if not impossible.

When we remember that these innate protective mechanisms are always ready in the background and understand how they work, there's plenty we can do to reboot our critical thinking skillfully when it freezes or our emotions go into a negative spiral. In this chapter, we'll explore several attention-based strategies you can try if you're overwhelmed or about to lose your cool. These strategies are useful both in meditation and daily life.

Do Nothing

Thoughts and emotions lead to more thoughts and emotions, and the more we try to control them, the more likely they are to spiral. If you're skeptical, try this thought experiment based on social psychologist Dan Wegner's work and see what happens.[2]

> Get comfortable and close your eyes.
> In a moment, I'll ask you not to think about a white bear for fifteen seconds. You can think of anything else, except for white bears.
> Ready?
> Close your eyes, rest, and for the next fifteen seconds DO NOT think about a white bear.
> How did it go?

If you're like the participants in Wegner's study, you found that the harder you tried not to think about a white bear, the more you thought about one, even if you had never thought about a white bear before. The takeaway? This thought experiment reveals that the more we try not to think about something, the more it comes to mind. Imagine how this natural domino effect of thoughts and emotions leading to more thoughts and emotions can be detrimental when we're stressed, worried, or anxious. It's no wonder that sometimes the most effective way to work with overly busy minds and big feelings is to do nothing.

Meditation is a highly personal experience, so much so that I could make the argument that there are as many methods as there are meditators. One is called doing nothing or nonmeditation, where we allow our mind to be "as it is." The formal names for this method are open awareness and shamatha without support, where we patiently and gently let our mind rest without trying to change or fix anything. By merely resting, we hone our concentration and our awareness of the patterns that underlie how we relate to ourselves and the world. When it comes to meditation, allowing our mind to just be is as old-school as you can get.

It's not always easy to let the mind rest as it is though, especially when we're tired, hungry, sick, or stressed. We've seen that many of us are drawn to meditation because we want to fix or remove something, so it's natural to want to get rid of unpleasant thoughts, emotions, and sensations. We've also seen that struggling against our experience is problematic. The thought experiment to not think about a white bear demonstrates the adage that "what we resist persists." There are other reasons not to put up a fight, too. When we struggle against our emotions, it's easy (and common) to demonize them instead of recognizing thoughts and emotions for what they are—valuable bits of information that don't reflect the whole picture. Battling with big feelings can shut us off from meaningful intuitions about what's happening within and around us that are embedded in the emotions themselves—intuitions around the safety, wholesomeness, or the trustworthiness of a person or situation, for instance. What's more, when we battle against our experience, we go to war against ourselves, often piling layers of self-criticism or judgment on top of the pressure we already feel. It's an act of self-compassion to stay with what's arising instead of battling with it. From Christopher Germer's pioneering book *The Mindful Path to Self-Compassion*:

> Compassion comes from the Latin roots *com* (with) and *pati* (suffer), or to "suffer with." When we offer genuine compassion, we join a person in his or her suffering. Being compassionate means that we recognize when someone is in pain, we abandon our fear of or resistance to it, and a natural feeling of love and kindness flows toward the suffering individual. The experience of compassion is the complete abandonment of the inclination to resist emotional discomfort. It's *full* acceptance: of the person, of the pain, and of our own reactions to the pain.
>
> *Self*-compassion is simply giving the same kindness to ourselves that we would give to others.[3]

Through meditation, we recognize that minds are made up of countless interdependent bits and pieces of thoughts, emotions, and sensations that are always in flux. Struggling against this fundamental nature of our minds is counterproductive, but we do it anyway even though there's no upside. If we stop expecting the nature of mind to be different than it is, then we can stop struggling against it. Doing so is a powerful expression of kindness and self-compassion. From there, we can learn to work with our minds, natural tendencies with attention, balance, compassion, and playfulness. We can investigate our self-talk with curiosity and a sense of humor without getting lost in its content or beating ourselves up. We can pay attention to our inner dialogue and the tone of our voice. Is it harsh and critical? Is it gentle and kind? Do we speak to ourselves the way we would a close friend? If not, we can change our internal tone to one that's more understanding and compassionate. Ultimately, we can reach the point where we don't identify with that voice anymore; it's nothing more than a leftover from our past conditioning. Until then, treating ourselves with kindness and compassion softens the effect of our inner voice when it's judgmental.

When we meet the workings of our minds and hearts with balance and good cheer without trying to eliminate or change them, our unpleasant thoughts, emotions, and sensations move through us more quickly. Then we feel more peaceful and at ease. Doing nothing in the context of meditation doesn't mean we no longer work to change unhelpful emotional patterns that contribute to our stress. It just means we do so patiently with the understanding that however powerful our thoughts and emotions are at any given moment, they're continually changing. Over time, we learn to treat ourselves with greater kindness and love.

Focus on What's Good

Given the pressure many of us are under, it's unrealistic to expect we'll always have the mental bandwidth to hold back from overanalyzing what's bothering us. We've seen how our natural tendency to think through problems interacts with the broader innate protective mechanisms that are always ready in the background to ensure survival. One of those survival mechanisms is a cognitive bias where we focus more on what feels threatening and dangerous than what's positive and uplifting. It's called a negativity bias, and that's what happens when we zero in on our problems and ignore what's good. It makes sense from an evolutionary perspective. In *Why Buddhism Is True*, author and journalist Robert Wright explains that "natural selection didn't design your mind to see the world clearly; it designed your mind to have perceptions and beliefs that would help take care of your genes." If we see a stick on the hiking trail ahead of us that looks like a rattlesnake, for example, we will react as if it's a rattlesnake even though it's a stick most of the time. Wright elaborates,

> This is an illusion in a literal sense: you actually believe there is something there that isn't there; in fact, you actually "see" it.
>
> These kinds of misperceptions are known as "false positives"; from natural selection's point of view, they're a feature, not a bug. Though your brief conviction that you've seen a rattlesnake may be wrong ninety-nine times out of a hundred, the conviction could be lifesaving the other one time in a hundred. And in natural selection's calculus, being right 1 percent of the time in matters of life or death can be worth being wrong 99 percent of the time, even if in every one of those ninety-nine instances you're briefly terrified.[4]

If we avoid just one rattlesnake bite, it's worth having recoiled from ninety-nine sticks. But if we leave a party, a business meeting, or a fun family event more focused on the snarky comment someone made about our new haircut than on the warm connections and overall good time we had, then being hardwired with a negativity bias seems more like an evolutionary disadvantage than an advantage.

Like all survival mechanisms, a negativity bias is meant to protect us, but it gets in the way if we react as if we're in danger when we're not or if it causes us to lose sight of what's good in our lives. Uplifting, joyful aspects of life exist side by side with challenging ones, but it's easy to focus more on what's going wrong than going right. It's worth the extra effort to acknowledge the challenge, then shift your attention to focus on what's good. Paying attention to positive experiences for as few as ten seconds helps to shift the way we think and feel away from a negative spiral. It also creates room for gratitude to emerge naturally. Couple positive thoughts with positive actions—like small random acts of kindness or appreciation—then, just as the children's book title *The Smile that Went Around the World* by Patrice Karst suggests, a chain reaction of kindness and appreciation can ripple out far and wide.

Shifting focus to take in the good is one of several anchor practices we use to ground ourselves by moving attention away from busy thoughts and big feelings to a pleasant or neutral object—a sound, phrase, image in our head, or sensation. Appreciation practices where we anchor our attention on what's good build concentration and are especially helpful when we're worried or upset. Focusing on what we're grateful for is different from feeling grateful, though. You may not feel grateful when you first practice appreciation. Don't worry if that happens to you. If you find yourself caught up in stressful or worrying thoughts, take a moment to notice them. Then, ask yourself if there's something you're grateful for, too. If there is, spend a moment taking that in. If nothing comes to mind, dig a little deeper and consider whether you're grateful for something that's often taken for granted—like your feet, your hands, or your beating heart.

Pay Attention to Something Else

Earlier we saw how relaxation activates the wing of the nervous system that promotes an expansive sense of ease and calm. When you relax and focus on the moment instead of thinking about the past or fretting about the future, some space opens in your head that makes room to consider options and make choices aligned with your motivation and values. By shifting your attention away from worrying thoughts and anxious emotions to something else, you can see what's happening within and around you more clearly, set priorities more confidently, and return to what you were doing with more balance. My son is a musician, and when he was a teenager, his go-to meditation practice was to put on headphones, listen to music, and focus on one aspect of the track—perhaps the bass line, the percussion, or the guitar. No one will find that instruction in a classical text, but it is a highly effective grounding strategy that settles your nervous system. (An added benefit of this practice is that it hones your concentration skills.) The most common grounding strategy is to shift your attention away from thoughts and emotions to physical sensations. Feel your feet against the ground, the breath in your belly, or your clasped hands. Can you soften and relax your muscles? Relaxing your body will often relax your mind.

WRAP-UP: Grounding Strategies to Steady Yourself

Minds don't always get busy, big feelings don't always bubble up, and bodies don't always get tense or restless when we meditate, but when that happens there's no need for concern. It's a normal part of practice. It's also normal to feel dull, bored, or distracted. Here are several attention-based anchoring strategies that make overly busy or bored minds, restless bodies, and big emotions more workable in meditation and daily life. When you use them, see if you can bring a sense of spaciousness and relaxation to the practice.

Attention-Based Grounding Strategies:
These anchor practices use our innate capacity
for attention to help us take care of ourselves

Focus on breath or sounds. If it's hard to relax, sit still, or focus, silently say "in" when you breathe in and "out" when you breathe out, or keep your attention on the sounds within and around you.

Appreciation. Take a gentle and patient look at the big picture and focus on a few good things in your life.

Breathe on purpose. Breathe in through your nose for four seconds, hold your breath for as long as you're comfortable doing so, then breathe out through your mouth for eight seconds. Repeat this a few times and see if you feel more settled.

Open your eyes. If your eyes are closed and big emotions feel overwhelming, open them.

Move. Big emotions or boredom can feel like restlessness or speedy energy. If that happens, move a little bit. Sway from side to side, walk, squeeze a pillow, rub your hands together, or shake your arms or legs to let go of the stressful energy.

Take a break. If you still feel restless or unsettled after trying these strategies, take a break. There is no shame in cutting a meditation short if you feel uncomfortable.

Compassion-Based Grounding Strategies: These anchor practices help us self-soothe by drawing on our innate capacity for kindness and compassion

Slogans. Slogans are phrases we recite silently or out loud. When we're stuck in a mental loop or when big emotions feel overwhelming, slogans help us ground and soothe ourselves. Two well-used helpful and compassionate slogans are "This is what it is right now" and "Right now, I'm okay." The words *right now* in both phrases remind us that everything is in flux and whatever's happening won't last forever. When we silently say, "This is what it is right now," we allow ourselves to feel our emotions rather than push them away. That doesn't mean we necessarily like what's happening, nor that allowing our feelings is the same as giving up. On the contrary, allowing means taking care of ourselves while holding in mind the maxim, "What we resist persists." When we silently say, "Right now, I'm okay," we hold back from worrying about what might go wrong later to remind ourselves that, even now, when we're not feeling great, there are ways in which we are okay.

Soothing and Supportive Touch. Soothing, supportive touch is a powerful way to practice self-love and self-compassion. You can find what comforts you by experimenting with a few of these ideas from Kristin Neff's book *Fierce Self-Compassion*:[5] Place one or both hands over your heart.

Place one hand over your heart, one hand on your belly,
and feel the movement of your breath.
Hug yourself.
Gently sway side to side or rock back and forth.
Squeeze one hand with the other.

WRAP-UP:
Allowing, Appreciation, and Self-Compassion

Struggling against our thoughts and big feelings is counter-productive and unkind. When we accept that they are natural manifestations of our minds and allow them to be, we give challenging thoughts and big feelings a chance to fade away on their own. Allowing them is a simple but not always easy act of self-compassion and self-care that helps us stay steady in medita-tion and in life.

Appreciation is also an act of self-compassion and self-care. Studies show that appreciation leads to more resilience by helping us remain optimistic and increasing our feelings of satisfaction when life is hard. It even strengthens our immune systems and promotes forgiveness and kindness to ourselves and others. The National Institutes of Health found that expressing gratitude improves relationship satisfaction by 26 percent! Remarkably, it doesn't take a lot of effort to experience these benefits.[6]

Practice

Make a mental list of several things you're grateful for and choose one of them—the one that feels most meaningful to you right now. Close your eyes for a moment, lower your shoulders, and settle into the movement of your breathing. Feel your breath as it moves in and out of your body. Now bring what you're grateful for to mind. Try not to analyze it; just be with it instead. When you're ready open your eyes.

Takeaway

If you're frustrated because something is not going the way you had hoped, reflect on something that's good in your life. See if broadening your perspective shifts the way you feel.

8

The Just-Right-for-Me Rule

Multiplicity, Interdependence, and Change

Earlier in my life, I used to work myself into a state of exhaustion, leaving no energy for me or my relationships. In college, I would study like crazy for exams and collapse when they were through. After graduation, I continued a less extreme version of this pattern at work and home. Wanting our family to experience my idea of iconic holiday celebrations, I'd juggle my day job with baking, shopping, cooking, cleaning, and decorating until I dropped. Same thing at work. I'd take on more than I could handle, push myself to the finish line, and then collapse. My favorite phrase for this is "crank and crash." It was my life for decades, and sometimes I left a mess in my wake. The maxim "We teach what we need to learn" was true for me. To lead a more balanced life, I needed to get smarter about three characteristics of the nature of my mind (and everything else)—multiplicity, interdependence, and change.

Finding what's just right for us might be the place in daily life where we see the relationship between multiplicity, interdependence, and change most directly. Here are some ways to view thoughts, emotions, and sensations to help us better understand their true nature.

Multiplicity. Thoughts, emotions, and sensations aren't just one thing. They are made up of many elements that combine, intermingle, and blend.

Interdependence. Thoughts, emotions, and sensations don't exist on their own. They cause and are caused by a changing range of experiences, only some of which we know or control.

Impermanence. Thoughts, emotions, and sensations continually change. They come and go. They get big and small. And they morph into something entirely different.

Stress and anxiety are normal. Too much of them, though, and we become overwhelmed. There's a level of pressure that is just right for you, where you have enough energy and focus to meet the needs of the task at hand without feeling swamped. What's just right for each of us depends on multiple factors as diverse as whether we're dehydrated, whether we're hot or cold, or whether our mood is happy or sad. These internal and external factors are interdependent, they are both the causes and effects of one another, and they're constantly changing. Finding the just-right response to internal and external circumstances is how we achieve balance in every aspect of our lives.

The name of the just-right-for-me rule harkens back to *Goldilocks and the Three Bears.* As the well-known story goes, when no one is there, a young girl with golden hair wanders through the home of three bears who live in a charming cottage in the woods. She tests the mama's, the papa's, and the baby bear's porridge, chairs, and beds to see which of them are just right for her—not too hot, not too cold, not too hard, not too soft. What's just right for Goldilocks or mama, papa, or baby bear differs. Goldilocks gets into some trouble for breaking and entering, but she isn't far off in trying to find a middle way that's just right for her.

In educational psychology, the just-right-for-me rule is similar to a learning model developed by psychologist Lev Vygotsky in the late 1920s called the zones of proximal development.[1] German educator Tom Senninger popularized the zones of proximal development for education in his Learning Zone Model, and Pema Chödrön reimagined them for meditators in her book *Welcoming the Unwelcome*.[2] All of these models are based on the principle that what's just right for us changes depending on internal and external conditions. Let's look at the three learning zones Senninger identified:

Comfort. In the comfort zone, things are familiar. It's where we perform well, set appropriate boundaries, rest, recharge, and reflect. It's not where we take risks or where much learning or growth occurs.

Challenge. In the challenge zone, our existing skills and abilities are within reach but stretched. There's enough pressure to motivate us, but not so much that we feel overwhelmed or panicked. (It's just right for us.) Here's where we build new skills that, once mastered, expand our comfort zone.

Overwhelm. Our challenges are more than we can handle when we're in the overwhelm zone. We feel chaotic, and our resources are depleted because we must manage our emotions while looking for safety and protection. Few (if any) resources are available for learning and growth.

Using learning zone terminology, we're in the overwhelm zone when our thoughts and emotions are in a negative spiral. Attention and compassion–based grounding strategies like the ones we explored in the last chapter help us stay in the challenge zone where we have the mental resources to learn and grow. Let's recap:

> Thoughts generate more thoughts; the more we think about our thoughts and emotions, the more of them we have. With awareness we notice this domino effect.
>
> With strong, stable attention we can stay in the challenge zone by interrupting the domino effect before our thoughts and emotions become a negative spiral.

It can be difficult to stay in the challenge zone when the present moment is messy. Earlier, we used the compassionate and soothing slogans "Right now, I'm okay" and "This is what it is right now" to befriend thoughts and emotions instead of struggling against them. Here are two additional slogans that encourage us to relate to our thoughts and feelings cheerfully—with a light touch and sense of humor.

Don't play the end of the scene before you get there. When we are worried about what will happen next, we are like actors who play the end of a scene before they get there. Actors know how their characters' stories will pan out, but for the audience to live the scene with them, actors cannot telegraph what will happen next. In real life, we don't know how a scene will end, but sometimes we think and act as if we do. The maxim "Don't play the end of the scene before you get there" reminds us not to get ahead of ourselves.

Drop your baggage. Revisiting the past is like hauling extra baggage that's heavy to carry. Anytime and anywhere, we can choose to drop the baggage and move forward less encumbered. Does this mean we forget what has happened in the past? No. Our minds and hearts are spacious enough to hold strong feelings without getting swept away by them.

Learning zones aren't fixed, nor are they like a light switch with only two settings: on and off. Learning zones, and the stress response that drives them, are more like a dimmer switch that gradually increases or decreases the light in a room. Or they are like the fader on a sound system that adjusts the volume up and down. Learning zones change along with us and depend upon our physical state. It's difficult to stay in the optimal challenge zone when we haven't gotten a good night's sleep, for example, or have a cold or are hungry (just like it's challenging to self-regulate). Learning zones also change with our emotional states. Our comfort and challenge zones narrow when we're stressed or upset. When we are aware of our physical and emotional states, we increase our agency over whether we slip into overwhelm, stay in the challenge zone, or move to the comfort zone.

Attention lets us notice when we're under pressure and where the dimmer switch is set. If the dimmer is set too high, we're inching toward the overwhelm zone or already in it, like when we're pushing hard to finish a project or to manage a sensitive issue at home. Then, attention-based strategies help us dial down the pressure. They also tell us when to dial it up, like when things at home or work require our attention but we don't have the energy to do them, so we binge-watch old television shows instead. Using attention-based strategies, we can dial up the pressure to increase our energy and move us out of our comfort zone into our challenge zone. When we feel challenged but not overwhelmed, we've found the just-right level of pressure for us—enough to push ourselves out of our comfort zones, but not so much that we slip into the overwhelm zone and shut down.

Unsurprisingly, the just-right-for-me rule also applies in our relationships. Our mental states are contagious, and people coregulate each other. Have you been at an event where someone new walked in and they sucked all the energy out of the room? It can happen before a single word is spoken. Or have you felt fine when you entered a room until you sensed tension among the people already there? You could tell that something was happening before anything was said, and you were affected by it. When an agitated person changes the dynamic, that person's nervous system is regulating us—not necessarily deliberately, but effectively. We don't need to be passive receivers of other people's stressful energy; when we are grounded, we can notice their tension without taking it on. The dynamic in the room might not change immediately, but the tide may turn eventually. Regardless, we will benefit from not becoming agitated.

We see the effects of coregulation in every relationship, including team development. In the mid-1960s, psychologist and researcher Bruce Tuckman developed a model of team development that is widely used today. (I was introduced to his work in Ruth King's excellent Mindful of Race yearlong program.[3]) Teams progress through five developmental stages that predict their internal dynamics and are most effective when members understand these stages. Tuckman created his model for project-based teams, but it applies to relationships across the board—friendships, marriages, and business partnerships, to name a few. The five stages of team development Tuckman identified are:

Forming

Storming

Norming

Performing

Adjourning/Transforming[4]

Earlier, we looked at what it takes to feel safe when engaging in inner work. That's also the central question in the initial forming stage of group development. The forming stage is often a honeymoon period, especially with teams where buy-in is already there and everyone believes in the mission. Even in the best of circumstances where people share common goals and values, conflict will ensue. All honeymoons end eventually, and when they do, relationships move to the storming stage of team development, where people navigate frustrations and disagreements. Not all relationships make it through the storming stage successfully. The ones where participants take the time to identify and reflect upon their safety and inclusion needs are more likely to weather the storms that inevitably emerge in any relationship.

If we take on the crucial task of identifying what it takes for us to feel safe and included during the forming stage of a relationship, we're less likely to project our own inclusion and safety needs onto someone else when we're in the storming stage. Often, we don't recognize that we're projecting, and neither does anyone else. As a result, everyone misses the real cause of a conflict: that someone's safety and inclusion needs are not being met. For instance, I thrive in a structured environment and feel uncomfortable when roles and expectations are fuzzy. I can take on extra tasks and responsibilities to create structure and organization without being asked. It took me some time to figure out that the primary reason I took on extra work was to ease my discomfort. I'm embarrassed to say that I mistakenly thought I was doing everyone a favor by taking the initiative and wanted them to appreciate my hard work! Other team members saw my taking the initiative differently; sometimes, they welcomed it, but other times they saw it as a play for control. Far from appreciating my initiative, they resented it. Meanwhile, I resented not being appreciated. A clear marker of a lose-lose situation is when everyone feels resentful. Resentment isn't good, but from a group dynamics perspective, there was a more significant issue. When I looked for the cause of the conflict externally, I couldn't identify my piece in it. When I saw and addressed the whole picture—both the internal and external causes of the conflict—I could better craft a lasting solution.

This dynamic can be avoided when we consider up front what it takes to feel safe and included. Hopefully, others will join the inquiry and create an environment where reflections around safety and inclusion are welcome and helpful. If no one else is game, reflecting on safety and inclusion needs is still worthwhile (like the ones we considered earlier in "Take Good Care"):

> What do you need to feel safe and included?
> Which of your safety and inclusion needs are being met
>   and how?
> What could be done to meet your unmet needs?

There's a well-known Buddhist story about tuning a lute or sitar. Tune the strings too tightly, and the notes you play will be sharp. Tune them too loosely, and the notes you play will be flat. Get the tension right, and your song will be in key. (It's the just-right-for-me rule again.) The lute metaphor is often used to demonstrate the importance of balancing effort and relaxation in meditation. It has broader applications, though, and can be used to reflect the middle ground between two poles on any spectrum. Or, as in the following example, tuning a lute also illustrates the ever-changing complexity around the question, "What does it take to feel safe?"

My husband can handle a level of external input that wears me down. Here's an example. One morning we got an email from friends who wanted to make plans, so we both looked at our calendars. I saw the number of days we had already booked and said we had a lot going on. Seth saw the number of open days and said we didn't have much going on. It was as if we were replaying a scene from Woody Allen's movie *Annie Hall*, where a therapist asks Woody Allen's girlfriend in the film (played by Diane Keaton), "How often do you have sex?" She responds, "All the time, THREE times a week!" In a parallel scene, the therapist asks Allen the same question. He answers, "Hardly ever, THREE times a week!"[5]

The difference in our perspectives around making plans is typical, and it's not usually a big deal. But that morning, adding something to our calendar felt like a big deal to me. When it comes to making plans, Seth's and my comfort zones can be different. Having a lot of advance plans puts him in his comfort zone and can take me out of mine. We have internalized this dynamic, and it usually doesn't trigger us. But that morning I was still recovering from surgery, and overbooking our calendar dialed up the stress and vulnerability I was already feeling. Whether the number of plans on the calendar was a lot or a little was not an objective fact. It was subjective depending on our points of view, and our points of view were in flux. On a different day and under other circumstances, our individual senses of whether our schedule was crowded or open could have been reversed. That day, my perspective was fueled by a concern for safety that may or may not have been justified. To paraphrase one of Tsoknyi Rinpoche's hallmark teachings, "It felt real, but that didn't mean it was true."[6] Too much reliance on safety and we're stuck in our comfort zones, leaving no room for growth. Stick our necks out too far, and we set ourselves back. When Seth and I were scheduling plans that morning, moving out of my comfort zone felt more like a risk than a stretch.

The solution to conflicts like this one is to find the sweet spot or middle ground, but here's what makes that tricky: the sweet spot we find today might not be our sweet spot tomorrow. Take Seth's and my difference of opinion over scheduling. Now, a crowded schedule is inconvenient and sometimes annoying, but I no longer feel stressed and vulnerable. If the same thing happened today, I doubt there would have been an issue, which brings us back to the lute metaphor. Why and when a lute needs tuning depend on multiple interdependent and ever-changing factors. When we know a lute is out of tune, addressing that is simple. When we recognize why we feel uncomfortable, addressing the problem is usually as straightforward as tuning a lute. Unfortunately, it's not always apparent that the reason we are uncomfortable is that we don't feel safe.

Tuning a lute is also a fitting metaphor for applying the just-right-for-me rule to being busy. We're not necessarily overwhelmed when we're busy. Despite the physical and psychological downsides of being too busy, there is a level of busyness that's healthy and good for us. Healthy pressure feels purposeful. When we're meaningfully engaged, we strengthen our cognitive skills. We're more focused, our brain circuits light up, and we can experiment with new ideas. That's what it means to be healthy busy— it's the just-right level of busyness. When we're healthy busy, we're more likely to sleep better because we're tired when we go to bed. It's often easier to wake up on mornings when we're healthy busy because we look forward to what's ahead. Focusing on something other than ourselves when we're healthy busy can broaden our perspectives and ease our anxiety.

The opposite of being healthy busy is "crazy-busy," a term coined by author Brené Brown in her book *Daring Greatly*. Brown suggests that being crazy-busy is a universal numbing strategy that allows us to ignore what's going on in our lives and how we feel about it.[7] Being busy can be an excuse to shift into autopilot and ignore our problems. Being crazy-busy isn't the same as being stressed out for reasons outside our control. Unavoidable stress is like the first arrow in the Buddhist parable; it wears us down and can adversely affect our health. Being crazy-busy wears us down and can adversely affect our health, too. The difference is that crazy-busy is avoidable—it's the second arrow.

It's common to view being busy as laudable when our home or work environment equates busyness with productivity. Then, being a busy person can become part of our identity. When we identify with an abstract concept like being busy, we treat being busy as if it's concrete—something stable and independent from the rest of our lives and us. That's a problem because it's different from how things work. Remember the relationship between multiplicity, interdependence, and change? Multiple interdependent and changing elements make up everything, including being busy. We have various tasks, expectations, motivations, and rewards associated with what we do. We take on multiple roles, for instance. We can be both the client and the service provider on the same project—or student and teacher, colleague and boss, parent, partner, and friend. None of the parts, pieces, or roles that make up being busy stand alone. Each relates to and depends on one another like puzzle pieces. Unlike the pieces of a puzzle, though, the roles we take on morph and intermingle. The entire system is affected when just one element changes or drops out.

When we see being busy, or any life experience, as a changing, interdependent system of many elements, we have a better sense of how things really are. We are not numb to what's happening anymore. We don't have agency over all the pieces in the puzzle that contribute to our stress, but with patience and careful investigation, we can recognize the elements that we control. With a more nuanced perspective on the big picture, we can make choices that are just right for our families, colleagues, communities, and us. Numb and crazy-busy no more, we recognize that we're lifelong learners able to chart a course toward a way of being in the world that's aligned with our priorities.

WRAP-UP: Multiplicity, Interdependence, and Change

Everyone and everything is made up of many elements that depend on each other and change. In nature, seasons change; leaves fall and decompose into the earth; and everything depends upon the wind, water, air, and sun to grow. Our inner worlds mirror what happens in nature. Looking at our thoughts, emotions, and sensations, we see that they change, combine, intermingle, and depend upon each other too. Thoughts, feelings, and sensations rise and fall, get big and small, and morph. When we remember that everything is in flux, interdependent, and made of many elements, we become more sensitive to the nuance of what's happening within and around us and see ourselves in a broader context.

Practice

Become curious about the parts and pieces that make up a thought, emotion, or sensation in your formal meditation practice. Where do they begin and end? How many are there? How do the parts and pieces depend on one another and how do they change? When one of them changes or drops out, do the others stay the same? If your thoughts, emotions, or sensations dropped away, would anything remain?

Takeaway

Bring this practice into daily life by applying it to a story you tell yourself. Become curious about the parts and pieces that make up your version of something that happened to you or someone else. Which of the elements of the story depend on one another? Do the other elements change if you take one of them away? Does the whole story change? Is anything left?

9

Our Bodies and Surroundings Change Minds

Cause, Effect, and Interdependence

Trudging up a steep patch of a trail in the Santa Monica Mountains, I was puzzling out a sticky situation. Tilted forward and looking down, I noticed my hands were tightly clutching my walking sticks. My core wasn't engaged, and my hands bore too much of my weight. Tension is a harbinger of fatigue and injury, and I had had enough experience to know that this hike would be less taxing on my body if I relaxed. When I moved my attention away from my thoughts to the sensations in my hands, my tight grip eased, and everything shifted. Without thinking about it, I engaged the muscles in my core and stood upright instead of tilting forward. Savoring the feeling of sunlight on my face, I soaked in the spectacular surroundings. My body had lifted, and so had my spirits. I could enjoy the hike instead of grimly trudging up the hill.

There's a reason the finest thinkers throughout history have thought on their feet: *Solvitur ambulando* is a Latin phrase often attributed to St. Augustine of Hippo (354–430 B.C.E.) that translated means "It is solved by walking." St. Augustine borrowed the axiom from the Greek philosopher Diogenes the

Cynic who, during a philosophical debate with the ancient philosopher Zeno, demonstrated that motion is real by getting
up and walking.[1] Diogenes was not the only Greek living a few
hundred years before the Common Era to extol the benefits of
walking. The Greek physician Hippocrates, often called "the
father of Western medicine" and said to have lived to 104, also
wrote of the benefits of walking. The oft-cited quote attributed
to Hippocrates—"Walking is the best medicine"—is close to the
actual text if not exact.[2] Aristotle was also known for walking and
thinking. His habit of walking while lecturing was so well established that his school and its students were called Peripatetics
(Greek *peri*, "around," and *patein*, "to walk").[3] In the nineteenth
century, Friedrich Nietzsche wrote in *Twilight of the Idols*, a brief
primer on his own philosophy, "Only thoughts which come from
walking have any value."[4] Also in the nineteenth century, Søren
Kierkegaard praised walking in a letter to his niece:

> Above all, do not lose your desire to walk: every day I walk
> myself into a state of well-being away from every illness;
> I have walked myself into my best thoughts, and I know
> of no thought so burdensome that one cannot walk away
> from it. . . . [I]f one just keeps on walking, everything will
> be all right.[5]

More recently, in the twenty-first century, Frédéric Gros,
author of *A Philosophy of Walking*, says walking is a prime example
of the philosophy of the everyday that "[looks] at the questions of
eternity, solitude, time, and space. . . . But on the basis of experience. On the basis of very simple, very ordinary things."[6] Mindful

awareness looks at life's big questions through the lens of very simple, very ordinary experiences, too.

With approximately 10 percent of adults in the United States having a mobility disability with serious difficulty walking or climbing stairs, the centuries-long celebration of walking might be better described as a celebration of being ambulatory.[7] Our brains are affected by our surroundings—inside and outside—but getting out in nature and moving are unparalleled in promoting health and well-being. In his essay *Walking,* Henry David Thoreau reminds us that we are part of nature and encourages us to let nature work its magic on us.[8] Pioneering naturalist John Muir writes in his journals, "I only went out for a walk and finally concluded to stay out till sundown, for going out, I found, was really going in."[9] Perhaps one of the reasons the beneficial effect of getting out in nature and moving has stood the test of time is that it embodies two universal themes woven through wisdom traditions: cause and effect and interdependence.

Our Bodies Change Our Minds

Growth and change are not linear; they are more like spirals, with each layer offering an opportunity to refine our experience and understanding. Meditation training has long used a spiral learning framework to help us progress from a surface understanding of our minds, bodies, and surroundings to a subtler one. We first investigate the outer or surface level by focusing on information from our five senses. Next, we consider what's happening on a subtle level by exploring the thoughts and emotional patterns that emerge in response. Last, we take an even more nuanced look by reflecting on what our sensory information and emotional responses to an experience tell us about the nature of our minds and reality. Investigating the nature of anything using this three-part progression from the surface to subtle to subtler still is like peeling an onion down to its core. Using repetition as a method, we deepen our understanding each time we revisit the experience. Working with this progression is as effective a tool to investigate our bodies and surroundings as it is to investigate our minds. Take posture, for example.

Binge-watching the ABC network's television show *Grey's Anatomy* was the first time I heard that striking a "superhero pose" could improve outcomes. (When the character Wonder Woman, from the eponymous and iconic DC comic book series, presses her fists into the small of her back, her shoulders and heart open, and her chin lifts—that's the superhero pose.) In episode fourteen of *Grey's Anatomy's* eleventh season (as of this writing, there have been nineteen seasons of *Grey's Anatomy*, making it one of the longest-running scripted series in television history), Amelia Shepherd, a young, spectacularly stunning neurosurgeon and head of surgery at the fictional Grey Sloan Memorial Hospital, is scrubbing in before performing brain surgery. Alone in the scrub room, she strikes a superhero pose. Moments later, another young, remarkably stunning neurosurgeon, Stephanie Edwards, joins her. Their exchange goes like this:

Stephanie: What is happening?
Amelia: I'm being a superhero.
Stephanie: Okay.
[Awkward pause.]
Amelia: There's a scientific study that shows if you stand like this, in superhero pose, for just five minutes before a

job interview or a big presentation or a really hard task, you will not only feel more confident, you will perform measurably better.

Stephanie: Seriously?

Amelia: Seriously.

[With her feet shoulder-width apart and hands in relaxed fists, Stephanie puts a fist on each side of the small of her back. Her head naturally lifts when she pulls back her shoulder blades.]

Amelia: You feel it?

Stephanie: We're superheroes.

Amelia: We are superheroes.[10]

The scientific study referenced here was conducted in 2012 by social psychologist and researcher Amy Cuddy and her colleagues at Harvard University. The study is also the subject of the second most-viewed TED Talk of all time, with about seventy million views as of this writing. The premise of Cuddy's study and TED Talk is that standing tall and taking our place in the world affects how we feel about ourselves, interact with others, and perform. Cuddy asked half the study's participants to strike an expansive posture and hold it for a few minutes before completing a task. She asked the other half to fold into a contracted posture before the task. Those who struck an expansive pose felt more powerful, took greater risks, and performed better in a mock interview. Following her extraordinarily successful TED Talk, Cuddy was the subject of unusually harsh criticism. Skeptics questioned the positive effect of power posing, specifically the hormonal effects that Cuddy reported. Eighteen years later, in a 2020 meta-analysis (a statistical summary of seventy-three studies), Cuddy's findings were validated, except for the hormonal effects. From the author of the meta-analysis, Mia Skytte O'Toole, a professor at Aarhus University in Denmark: "[I]t is non-controversial to say that the way we approach the world with our physical bodies shapes the way we think and feel."[11] Cuddy offers this takeaway toward the end of her TED Talk:

Our bodies change our minds
. . . and our minds change our behavior
. . . and our behavior changes our outcomes.[12]

The premise that posture affects outcomes jibes with what contemplatives tell us about the nature of reality—that everything is interdependent because it results from cause and effect. We see this firsthand when we meditate. A classical meditation instruction on posture goes something like this:

It's okay if you cry but keep your posture.
It's okay if you laugh but keep your posture.
It's okay if your mind is busy and won't settle down but
    keep your posture.

No one feels steady and robust all the time—absolutely no one. Meditators may not feel like superheroes when tears fall down their cheeks or they unsuccessfully hold back a laughing attack, but they often feel better for it. The aim of the meditators' version of "Keep calm and carry on" is to stay with what shows up in their experience instead of getting carried away by it. What do meditators do if they cry, laugh, feel restless, or are overwhelmed? They keep their posture and fake it, but not like the controversial aphorism

"Fake it till you make it." They fake it until they internalize the principle that time is their ally when it comes to big feelings. If they hold on, "This too will pass." As is often the case with clichés, there is a germ of truth in these three common ones.

When I was growing up, my parents encouraged me to stand tall because my posture would affect what others thought of me. I only cared a little about how others viewed me then, so their reasoning could have been more persuasive. Years later, in yoga and Pilates classes, I saw that good posture changes how I feel and view myself for the better. Decades later still, posture was the focus of my physical therapy after heart surgery. The degree to which my movements are connected to the small core muscles below my nonexistent six-pack and the muscles between my shoulder blades was a revelation. So was learning that by inadvertently jutting my chin forward I was compromising my posture. These insights have changed how I move through the world quite literally. As a result, I pay close attention to how I "hold my carriage" when I walk to the subway or down a flight of stairs. My parents' surface understanding of posture was about as basic as it gets. It took me the better part of my lifetime to recognize and internalize a subtle understanding of how posture affects the way I feel, as well as how I relate to others, myself, and my surroundings.

Me trudging up the hiking trail is an example of how someone can progress from a surface understanding of something to one that's more nuanced, then to an even subtler understanding. Cause, effect, interdependence, and change are part of every experience, and tiny adjustments to our physical, emotional, and behavioral patterns yield big results. My spirits lifted when my body lifted, partly because my posture improved. But there was more to it than that. I stopped looking at my feet when I engaged my core and my shoulder blades automatically pulled back. With my head held high, I could take in the spectacular surroundings and drink up the sunlight. Awareness of my posture and adjusting it helped me feel better physically and emotionally. Awareness of my surroundings not only helped me to feel better, but it also had a ripple effect. No longer looking down, I could relate to the other hikers on the trail more naturally. When we passed each other, we would often smile and say hello.

Our Surroundings Change Our Minds

The connection between a person's surroundings and their well-being is well established. In *The Extended Mind*, a remarkable survey of how our thinking processes are not limited to what happens in the brain, acclaimed science writer Annie Murphy Paul writes, "All of us think differently depending on where we are." She continues, "The field of cognitive science commonly compares the human brain to a computer, but the influence of place reveals a major limitation of this analogy: where a laptop works the same way whether it's being used at the office or while we're sitting in a park, the brain is deeply affected by the setting in which it operates."[13] Consider clutter. Studies of living in messy and disorganized spaces link clutter to procrastination, emotional exhaustion, reduced executive functioning, and more snacking. Wives living in cluttered homes have higher stress levels and are more depressed than their husbands. A messy environment impairs people's judgment, increases the odds that they will act impulsively, and makes interpersonal connections more difficult.

It's not just the stuff in our surroundings that affect us, though. The light, sound, smell, and temperature of our external environments also affect our health, mood, and performance.[14]

No natural aspect of our surroundings has a more significant effect on us than light, which synchronizes our biological clocks to wake us up, keep us focused, and help us sleep. "The circadian clock is the internal timing system that interacts with the timing of light and food to produce our daily rhythms," writes researcher Satchin Panda in his trailblazing book *The Circadian Code*.[15] Most parts of the brain and the body's organs have an internal clock that dictates circadian rhythms and forms the foundation of good health. It is our circadian rhythms that optimize our biological functions. Light and darkness synchronize the circadian rhythms in our brains while what we eat synchronizes the rest of our bodies' biological clocks. When our internal clocks are synchronized, our immune systems are more effective. When they are disrupted, the effectiveness of our immune systems is dampened. Frequent disruptions lead to health issues like insomnia, sleepiness, lack of energy, and depression. Extended disruptions lead to more significant health risks like obesity, diabetes, heart disease, and stomach problems. The light we see with our own two eyes connects our circadian rhythms to the outside world.

That my spirits lifted when I was hiking and felt the sun on my face would likely come as no surprise to Panda, who, in an interview for the *Economist*, explains, "[Light] affects so much of our psychology, physiology, and mood. But we take it for granted."[16] Suicide attempts and rates of depression increase in the winter months in places where the nights are long. Sunny environments can ease depression and physical pain. The beneficial effect of natural light on health and well-being makes obvious sense—light in the morning cues us to wake up, and darkness at night cues us to wind down. The negative effect of artificial light is less obvious, though, especially the negative effect of the blue light from our digital devices.

Light includes all the colors on the spectrum, but to synchronize our biological clocks, our eyes mostly pick up blue, green, and red. Blue light has the most significant effect on our circadian clock. The high level of blue light in the morning sun signals our body to wake up, while the lower levels of blue light at dusk signal it to wind down. Through the nineteenth century, when our light sources were fire and sun, bright light in the evening was rare and most people went to bed close to sunset. Everything changed with the introduction of artificial light sources—task lighting like lamps, overhead lighting like fluorescents, and digital lighting in smartphones and computers. These artificial light sources have high intensities of blue light that trick our brain into thinking it's daytime when it's not. "We evolved to be blue sensitive, we need it," explains Panda in his *Economist* interview. Timing of blue light exposure matters, though, and the worst time for us to take it in is before going to sleep.

Panda and other researchers offer clear, practical advice for using light and darkness to synchronize our circadian rhythms and support good health. Here are a few of their tips.

With the motto, "sunlight before screen light," neuroscientist and podcaster Andrew Huberman encourages us to get outside every morning and take in the sun. Five to thirty minutes of morning light, depending on whether it's a bright or sunny day, triggers our body to release "wake-up hormones," one of which is cortisol. Cortisol gets a bad rap, but at the appropriate time and level, it is essential for energy and immune function. Timing matters when it comes to sun exposure. A cortisol release needs to arrive early in the day for us to get the most out of it. "If you don't get sunlight early in the day," says Huberman, "that cortisol release starts shifting later, which creates issues with insomnia and anxiety and even some low-level depression later in the day. Now, that does not mean that if you miss getting sunlight one day that you're going to get depressed. It's a slow, integrated mechanism." *Note: sitting by a window isn't as effective as going outside. The glass filters out some of the beneficial ultraviolet light that synchronizes our brains' internal clocks. So do sunglasses.*

To synchronize our biological clocks with the outside world, Panda recommends we spend at least thirty minutes every day outdoors. To help us sleep at night, he recommends reducing exposure to bright indoor light and digital screens for two to three hours before going to bed.[17]

Skygazing and Stargazing

Meditators have long rested in the daylight while skygazing and in the darkness of night while stargazing. In Tibet, caves are used just for that purpose; when you look out from the cave, you can't see anything other than the sky! Skygazing and stargazing remind us to connect with the skylike nature of our minds and hearts. Just as the vast sky above us has the space to hold whatever moves through it, the vast skylike nature of our hearts and minds has the space to hold all that we experience without getting swept away. When skygazing and stargazing, we see how the activity in our minds, bodies, and surroundings cause and affect one another and are constantly changing. Remembering that mental activities like these are transient and interdependent helps us develop a humbler, more open perspective. Then, when we investigate our inner and outer worlds, we're better able to keep our sense of humor and take things a little less personally.

Skygazing and stargazing also help us develop the mental muscle to look beyond thoughts and emotions to see the long view. Like a telescope or pair of binoculars, this meditation method allows us to look past what is in front of us to find the big picture. This skill is especially helpful when our feelings are hurt or if we are stuck on something like a personal insult or a slight. When skygazing and stargazing, like with other practices, we don't ignore thoughts, emotions, and sensations or pretend they don't exist. We include them in our skylike awareness along with everything else. When our perspective is as vast as the sky, there's plenty of room for the full range of life's joys and sorrows.

WRAP-UP: Cause, Effect, and Interdependence

Nothing happens without an effect. Whether it's a good deed, a misdeed, or anything in between, everything springs from causes and conditions. Some causes and conditions are within our control, and others are not. We know about some of them, but not about others. In basic Buddhist philosophy, this is what interdependence looks like and why nothing in daily life is a separate, unified entity.

Classical meditation training commonly uses a three-part sequence to investigate life experiences. We start with a surface exploration by considering the information we glean through our five senses. The second level of investigation is subtler, moving from sensory impressions to our thoughts and emotional reactions to the experience. The last level of investigation looks at even subtler aspects of the experience like cause and effect, interdependence, multiplicity, and change.

Practice 1

Find a comfortable seat where you can see the sky without looking directly into the sun. Close your eyes. Inhale and exhale once, twice, and now for a third time. Let your body and mind settle at their own pace, without manipulation or analysis. When you're ready, open your eyes and gaze at the horizon or gaze directly into the sky but away from the sun. You don't need to meditate; just look into the vast open sky. Do you see a beginning or an end? Is there an inside or an outside? Allow thoughts and emotions to come and go as you remain present and undistracted. There's nothing for you to figure out or understand, just rest in the skylike nature of your mind. Don't overthink this practice. Most people have practiced skygazing or stargazing on their own, even if they didn't know they were doing it—staring into space outside in nature or in their living rooms. *Note: Skygazing is one way to integrate Huberman's fifteen minutes of morning light rule into your routine. If you prefer doing something more active first thing in the morning, try practicing yoga or tai chi outdoors.*

Practice 2

Choose one of the following: posture, light, or your surroundings. Pay attention to your choice without trying to change, fix, or eliminate anything. Look for a surface understanding by noticing what you learn about your choice through your five senses. Then, look for a more nuanced understanding by bringing awareness to your thoughts, feelings, and opinions about it. Last, dig deeper still for a subtler understanding by considering the causes, effects, interdependence, and changing nature of what you noticed. After reflecting on what you learned through this investigation, consider how you might skillfully adjust your relationship to the option you chose—posture, light, or surroundings—to live a healthier and more balanced life. If you find this practice helpful, repeat it with the other two options.

Takeaway

When faced with a dicey situation, reflect on its causes and effects. You'll be able to identify some but not all of them. Are the causes and effects interdependent? Do they have multiple elements that change?

10

Steady like a Log

Concentration and Discernment

We can uncover all we need to know about the nature of mind and reality by patiently and carefully investigating what's happening inside and out with steady concentration. Concentration is a central element in formal meditation training. My formal training has been mostly in Tibetan Buddhism, where imagination practices like visualization open the door to an unlimited range of experiences, some that we know and others we can only imagine. Imagination is used to hone concentration, especially in Vajrayana. It is not the most common method for training concentration, though. Most meditation systems emphasize calm abiding meditation, like the anchor practices we looked at earlier. In the Mahamudra system, calm abiding practice is called *shamatha* in the Sanskrit language, and in the Theravada system, the same practice is called *samatha* using the Pali language. In this practice, a meditator collects their mind and brings it to a state of stillness and rest. When meditators use their calm, collected minds to investigate the mind itself, they glean insights into more than the nature of mind; they glean insights into everyone and everything.

It's tough to concentrate when our minds are caught up in judgments, opinions, or stories about what we're thinking, sensing, or feeling. In *The Relaxed Mind* Dza Kilung Rinpoche describes how classical meditation texts compare this state of mind to a wild animal that is out of control.[1] If you've ever felt like your mind is acting like a wild animal, you are not alone. Meditators have compared their minds to monkeys, bears, and wild elephants from as far back as the eighth century.

When you quickly shift focus from one thing to another, your mind is like a monkey swinging from tree to tree. Jumping from thought to thought, or toggling between several computer programs, is like swinging from one tree branch to another—useful for some things (like air traffic control) but lousy for sustained concentration.

When you're busy all day but don't get much accomplished, your mind is like a bear. The analogy goes like this: A bear is fishing in a river when a school of fish swims downstream. Excited by all the fish it sees, the bear grabs as many as it can as quickly as it can and throws them onto the riverbank. Rather than paying attention to the fish it has already caught, the bear keeps grabbing more fish and throwing them on the riverbank, too. While the bear's back is turned, the fish he had thrown onshore slide back into the river and swim away. The bear is so busy catching new fish that he doesn't notice that the ones he had already caught have escaped. After an afternoon of fishing, the bear is left exhausted with nothing to show for his effort.

When your mind races, like at night when you can't fall asleep, your mind is like a wild elephant. The harder you try to stop thinking, the more stubborn your thinking becomes.

I can't say with certainty that an untrained pet is happier after it's been trained, although many experts will tell you that's the case. But I will tell you that I am happier when my pets are trained, and that comparing my mind when it is restless and judgmental to an untrained animal is an analogy that rings true to me. The ancient meditators were on to something.

An age-old method for training a wild elephant is to tether it to a post with a rope. At first, the elephant will bolt and try to get away, but eventually it will settle down and rest peacefully. The elephant is like a distracted mind, pulling, bucking, and doing everything it can to resist settling down. If you're a parent, you've seen this behavior before—an exhausted child desperately in need of sleep doing everything in their power to avoid lying down to rest. The post is the anchor we focus on when we practice calm abiding meditation. It could be a sound, a sensation, an image in our head, or another neutral or pleasant object. The tether or rope is a clear intention to focus, coupled with the gentle, friendly effort that causes the elephant to stay. In meditation training, the tether is referred to as mindfulness. The more the elephant struggles against the rope, the less comfortable it becomes. Once the elephant recognizes that struggling makes matters worse, it gets with the program and stops pulling. In *The Way of the Bodhisattva*, one of the great epic poems of Mahayana Buddhism, Indian sage Shantideva explains:

If with mindfulness' rope,
The elephant of mind is tethered all around,
Our fears will come to nothing.
Every virtue [will] drop into our hands.[2]

My mind felt like a monkey, a bear, and a wild elephant on the first day of a meditation retreat I sat with Tsoknyi Rinpoche in 2015. Tsoknyi Rinpoche, Mingyur Rinpoche's older brother and one of Tulku Urgyen Rinpoche's four accomplished and highly esteemed sons, is a remarkable teacher with whom I've been fortunate to study. His wise and cheerful way of being in the world has had a significant effect on me. The retreat was at the Mount Madonna Center in Northern California, the same place where I had sat retreat with Kabat-Zinn and Santorelli years before. Rinpoche's retreats are typically six days long, with one two-and-a-half-hour teaching and four group meditation sessions each day. They are mostly in silence, which means that outside of the teaching sessions, people keep to themselves and refrain from talking on the phone or to one another. If your life is busy with work, family, or social obligations, a silent retreat is a rare, uninterrupted opportunity to hear the voices in your head and see them as they are. Newcomers to a silent retreat may think their minds will settle quickly and that it won't take long for them to feel calm and peaceful. But that's not always the case. It can take a while for our minds to settle on retreat, and the silence on the outside can make our inner voice sound cacophonous.

On this retreat, my inner voice was extremely conversational and wasn't interested in settling down because I was navigating a tricky situation in my life outside the retreat. A story would show up in my head and I'd get well into analyzing it before realizing I was lost in thought. The busyness of my mind didn't worry me, but its persistence was surprising. Concentration comes easily to me and usually I settle in quickly. That didn't happen at this retreat, though. In the meditation hall, in the dining room, in my cabin, and walking in the woods, my thoughts tumbled through my mind one after another like water cascading down a mountainside. Cascading thoughts are so common in meditation that "like a waterfall" is the first of three analogies used to describe the development of concentration in shamatha. In the thought experiment "Don't think about a white bear," we've seen what happens if we try to stop a waterfall of cascading thoughts. The waterfall of thoughts is a force of nature, and wanting our minds to be different than their natural state is like waging a war inside our heads. That kind of wanting is counterproductive and unkind. When we stop wanting our minds to be different than their natural state, we stop battling with ourselves. That's an act of kindness and compassion. Waging war isn't an appealing idea, especially with ourselves, but please indulge me to puzzle this out with you.

If your mission is to battle back thoughts until your mind is calm, like how a wild elephant struggles against the tether that ties it to a post, your mind is the battlefield. When you try to fix, change, or eliminate thoughts and emotions, you're acting like the wild elephant when it pulls against a rope. But battling with the rope doesn't calm the elephant nor does battling back thoughts calm your mind. It's only when the elephant stops fighting that it can settle down and rest. The same is true for your mind. Waging a battle against your thinking mind can keep thoughts and emotions going and strengthen them, taking you further from the steady, concentrated mind you seek. Shamatha meditation slows down our thinking processes and heightens awareness of the natural movement of our minds, making it easier to see how frequently we're distracted by thoughts, emotions, and sense impressions.

At first, shamatha can make our minds feel wilder because we're aware of thoughts and emotions that we hadn't noticed before and see how they spiral. How do we respond? Again, from Shantideva's epic poem, *The Way of the Bodhisattva,* we stay steady like a log:

> When the urge arises in the mind
> To feelings of desire or wrathful hate,
> Do not act! Be silent, do not speak!
> And like a log of wood be sure to stay.

A verse or two later in the poem:

> And when you want to fish for praise,
> Or criticize and spoil another's name,
> Or use harsh language, sparring for a fight,
> It's then that like a log you should remain.

Shamatha has two methods: one with support and another without support. (Shamatha without support is another name for open awareness, a method we've looked at already.) Shamatha with support is compared to a spotlight, and shamatha without support is compared to a floodlight. The spotlight (shamatha with support) is a stable stance of attention where meditators stay alert and undistracted as they direct their attention toward an object or anchor. The floodlight (shamatha without support) is a wide, receptive stance of attention that lights up a broad field of changing experience. Distinguishing one from the other is helpful when training new meditators even though they aren't entirely separate; the floodlight of attention includes the spotlight because the meditator must remain alert and undistracted while practicing it.

I had been meditating quite a while when I sat this retreat, and I knew how to practice shamatha. Because my mind was busy,

I thought my best bet would be to start by practicing shamatha with support—the spotlight of attention. With relaxed attention, I focused on an object (my breath, a sound), noticed when my mind wandered, then brought it back to the object gently. Repeat. Repeat again. And again. I followed that drill in and out of the meditation hall, but still my thoughts remained unruly, and my body was often tense. No matter how hard I tried, I couldn't stay steady like a log.

That which doesn't kill us makes us stronger. But what if that which doesn't kill us could soften our hearts too? This modification to Nietzsche's general rule is the aim of an ancient practice from the Mahayana system called lojong, brought to Tibet by the esteemed Indian yogi and scholar Atisha (more on Atisha later). Lojong training uses slogans—sometimes called aphorisms or phrases—to develop compassion and wisdom. It's based on the premise that we can use the obstacles that life sends our way to soften our hearts and strengthen our minds. One of the fifty-nine lojong slogans, "Turn all mishaps into the path," encourages us to see every experience—even challenging ones like the tricky situation I was navigating on that retreat—as an opportunity for growth and learning.

Several of the lojong slogans offer guidance on how to develop discernment—the ability to judge well. "Don't be swayed by external circumstances" reminds us not to be overly influenced by events or situations. Rather than being swayed by the surface-level appearances of something, this slogan reminds us to always look deeper. "Of the two witnesses, hold the principal one" is perhaps the most direct teaching on discernment from the lojong slogans. The first witness is what other people think, and the second is our take on what's going on. This well-used slogan suggests that when we pay close attention to what's happening within and around us, we strengthen our discernment. Then, we can be our own best guide.[3]

When a meditator's inner voice is loud and unruly, one way for them to exercise discernment is by choosing their method skillfully. There are concentration methods other than shamatha that focus your mind, and I tried several of them on that retreat. I practiced appreciation, exchanging one type of thought for another. When thoughts about the tricky situation I was navigating popped into my head, I reminded myself of all the good in my life and the lives of those I love. I practiced love and compassion for the other people involved in my challenging situation by imagining what it would be like to walk in their shoes. Then, in my imagination, I exchanged myself for them. I offered love and compassion to myself by picturing a ladle of compassionate nectar and imagining how it would feel were I to pour it over my head. I stretched, moved, and walked in nature during our breaks to give my body a chance to release stressful energy and relax. These methods helped me settle down some of the time, but not all of it.

Another way meditators exercise discernment is by finding the balance between making too much effort and not enough. It's the lute metaphor and the just-right-for-me rule again. Too much effort can backfire, leading our minds and bodies to become tense and restless. If we relax too much, we risk falling asleep. The gold standard is to practice with relaxed, minimal effort—just enough effort so that the meditator is alert while remaining at ease. Even for experienced meditators, finding the right balance between effort and relaxation is out of reach sometimes. It takes discernment to know when to shift gears or take a break. In his book *Secret of the Vajra World*, Reggie Ray explains:

The most important point in the practice of shamatha is this: the level of heavy-handedness of the technique must match the level of the grossness of one's conceptual activity; the technique, in the degree of effort required, must be commensurate with the degree of conceptuality that one is experiencing. A light technique applied to heavy conceptuality will get nowhere. A heavy technique applied to very little conceptuality will itself generate more conceptuality than was there in the first place. The adjustment must be appropriate and skillfully applied.[4]

On the first night of that retreat, alone in my cabin and far from home, my mind grew unruly again, and I had trouble sleeping. My first few hours of sleep were fitful, then I woke in the middle of the night tired, frustrated, and a little bit mad. I was worried I wouldn't be able to go back to sleep and I'd be exhausted the next day. I decided to shift gears and try a somewhat "heavy-handed" concentration method that classical meditation texts describe as "crushing mind with mind itself" where meditators block thoughts and emotions rather than include them.[5] When coupled with a light touch and sense of humor, this method can be very effective. Had I been at home with my usual responsibilities and routine, a discerning response to a meditation session as challenging as this one might have been to take a break rather than power through. I hope I would have taken a break instead of powering through had it been my first silent residential retreat, too. But that week, I had no other obligations and plenty of retreat experience. There was no downside to my giving a slightly "heavier-handed" technique a try. I powered up the spotlight of my attention and, to the exclusion of all else, focused on the sensations in my lower legs and feet. Keeping my thoughts and feelings at bay, I felt my legs and feet sink into the mattress. Eventually, I was able to relax and sleep.

WRAP-UP: Concentration and Discernment

The spotlight and floodlight of attention are two ways to develop relaxed concentration. Much like a flashlight pointing at a single flower in a spring meadow at night, we use the spotlight of our attention (shamatha with support) to shine a light on a particular aspect of our experience, like our breath, a sound, or a visualization. The spotlight mode of attention enhances our focus and allows us to emotionally regulate, manage distractions, and accomplish daily tasks. Like a floodlight that lights up a whole swath of flowers in a spring meadow at night, we can also broaden our attention to a more receptive mode that takes in the breadth of our experience—one called open awareness or shamatha without support. With the floodlight mode of attention, we are open to the full range of sensations, feelings, sounds, and thoughts that come and go. The floodlight of attention invites openness, creativity, insight, and playfulness into meditation and daily life. With experience and practice, we develop the discernment necessary to choose which meditation technique to apply and for how long. With discernment, we also identify when it makes sense to take a break.

Practice

Experiment with the spotlight and the floodlight modes of attention. Let's say you're sitting on a sofa that faces a bookshelf. Inhale, gently hold your breath, soften your forehead, soften your jaw. Exhale as you lower your shoulders. Breathe naturally for a few breaths and lightly focus on your exhale. When you're ready, softly gaze at a single title on the shelf. Keeping your body still and without straining, look at the book carefully to take in the details. How is it bound? What color is it? Check out the book's spine. Focus on the font. Without changing your physical position and still looking ahead, expand your gaze to include a few other books and take them in. Broaden your gaze further to include the whole shelf. In the same position and with your body still, include as much of your peripheral vision as possible without changing your physical position. Rest there for as long as you like.

Takeaway

Test-drive this practice in daily life. If something catches your eye (a plant, for instance), focus on a single bloom or leaf first and then broaden your field of vision progressively to include neighboring leaves, the entire plant, and your surroundings.

11

So Be It

Awareness and Allowing

My husband is a great storyteller and so are many of his friends who are also writers. When they get together, they sometimes tell funny stories about working on television shows. One of my favorites is told by John Romano who, besides being a former college professor and screenwriter, wrote on hit television shows for many years. This story is about a telephone meeting he once had with Leonard Goldberg, a successful television producer who also had a hand in producing many blockbuster movies. Romano talks about this meeting as if singing in an opera with his aria a single, extended crescendo. Here's my version of his story.

The year was 1993, and Romano was finalizing the scripts on a show he had created for 20th Century Fox, a television studio Goldberg was running at the time. The show was called *Class of '96* and was already in production. Goldberg always wanted a look at a script before it was filmed to talk about what changes needed to be made. It was getting close to time to shoot the episode, and he hadn't yet weighed in on the script. Romano tracked him down and learned that, on the recommendation of friends, Goldberg had gone to Las Vegas to see Cirque du Soleil. So Romano called the hotel where he and his wife were staying. When the switchboard put him through to their room, the actor Michael Caine answered in his unmistakable Cockney accent. He was the friend who had recommended the Goldbergs see Cirque du Soleil! Goldberg came to the phone and told Romano that he had read the script on the plane. He was complimentary. Then he began to give Romano notes. Extensive ones. An hour later, Romano tried to change the subject by asking Goldberg if he had enjoyed Cirque du Soleil. "Not my cup of tea," Goldberg replied, "Let me describe it for you."

A high-wire artist walks a tightrope suspended twenty-five feet above the stage without a safety net. He's balancing a pole on his shoulders with a man sitting on each end of the pole. To underscore the point, the tightrope walker isn't just walking a highwire without a safety net, he's doing it while carrying a man on each shoulder. Each of the men on the high-wire artist's shoulders also carries a pole on his shoulders with a man on each end of the pole. The high-wire artist is walking a tightrope carrying not just two men on his shoulders but six men on his shoulders. And that's just the beginning! The men on the shoulders of the two men on the high-wire artist's shoulders are also carrying poles on their shoulders. On each end of each of those poles, there's a man carrying a pole on his shoulders. The high-wire artist is carrying not just six men as he walks a tightrope that's twenty-five feet in the air, he's carrying fourteen men. All without a safety net!

Goldberg was a great man in the entertainment industry known for his invaluable insights, and Romano was eager to hear the moral of this story. Goldberg told him, "Let's say for the sake of argument they're the best in the world at this." He paused for dramatic effect. Then with a lilt in his voice and a flourish, Romano, who was relating the story, imitated Goldberg who said, "Who gives a shit?"

....

I woke up for the second full day of retreat exhausted.

....

Generally, the early morning hours are a rich time for me. It's the time of day that I usually connect with a concentrated and even blissful mental state easily. But my mind was already revved up in the early morning meditation on the second full day of that retreat, before breakfast and after a lousy night's sleep. Frustrated, tired, and hungry, I was fed up with the whole idea of meditation, until I remembered these lines from "Go to the Limits of Your Longing," by Rainer Maria Rilke, a Bohemian-Austrian poet and novelist.

Let everything happen to you: beauty and terror.
Just keep going. No feeling is final.[1]

I let go of my attempts to concentrate and allowed my thoughts to run wild. The voice in my head quickened and grew louder. I didn't have the energy to practice any strategies. I didn't have the energy to think about and analyze what my inner voice was saying either, even though reflecting on my thoughts is something I find helpful sometimes. My intuition told me I needed a rest, and my body took over. My shoulders lowered, my jaw and forehead softened, and eventually my mental activity slowed down. My thoughts weren't cascading like water down the side of a mountain anymore; instead, they moved evenly and slowly like water flowing down a river. A mighty river is the second of the three analogies classical teachings use to describe the stages of Mahamudra shamatha. In his book *Contemplating Reality*, teacher, author, and photographer Andy Karr compares the first and second stages of shamatha to driving a car:

> Eventually you start to see that there are different ways of slowing down. If you are driving too fast in your car, you can hit the brakes or you can simply lift your foot from the gas. When we start to meditate, there is a natural tendency to try to find the brakes, but in the long run we learn that there are no brakes nor anyone to put their foot down. We might succeed at suppressing thoughts and emotions for a while, but at the price of binding the mind further. We start to see that the best way of practicing shamatha is to take your foot off the gas while staying mindful. You learn to rest right within the very things that disturb you. You start to work with the energy of mind rather than struggling against it. This brings stability to your practice.[2]

For most of the remaining ninety-minute session, I watched the same stories, with their various characters dressed up in different costumes circling my mind, but I held back from interfering with them. Toward the end of the session, my stories were interrupted by different voice in my head. It wasn't mine but Romano's, with its unmistakable lilt and flourish, saying, "Who gives a shit?" It was as if the release valve on a pressure cooker had flipped open or the dam that had been holding back my sense of humor had broken. The stories I had been telling myself lost their hold on me; I recognized they had no substance and some were ridiculous. Thoughts and stories still bubbled up, but they didn't disturb my peacefulness. I felt a deep sense of calm, connection, and relief.

The analogy classical teachers use to describe the third stage of shamatha is that the mind becomes like an ocean. Now I had the mental bandwidth and physical ease to practice a different meditation method in the Mahamudra system called *vipashyana* (*vipassana* in the Theravada system). This method develops insight and is central to investigation. With my mind more at rest, I could shift emphasis from steadying my mind with shamatha's concentration practice to investigating my mind with vipashyana's insight practice. Thoughts and emotions don't disappear when your mind is like an ocean; they're like ripples on the surface. We notice them and let them run their course. That can take some intestinal fortitude. Thoughts and emotions are powerful, even though they're temporary, but if you let them, they'll move on. Only by allowing thoughts and emotions to rise and fall do we develop the confidence to leave them alone. That doesn't often happen the first time we give it a try; it takes patience and practice.

Romano's irreverent and joking voice became my meditation buddy for the rest of that retreat. When a mental story threatened my peacefulness, the mantra "Who gives a shit?" bubbled up and grounded me. This silly mantra lightened my mood and made me smile. Please don't be mistaken: this was a critical time in my life, and I sincerely cared about what was happening outside of retreat. But that was different from the stories that ran through my head while I was sitting retreat. There was a flavor of real life in those stories, but they were also fueled by projections that could carry me away. The good-humored mantra "Who gives a shit?" reminded me not to take myself too seriously. The insight it offered pointed me toward a less conceptual mental space, one that was grounded in my body.

I doubt that it's a coincidence that I remembered Romano's story while sitting a retreat with Tsoknyi Rinpoche because Rinpoche is known for a mantra that is like Romano's. In the Buddhist magazine *Lion's Roar*, Rinpoche writes:

> [R]aise your arms to shoulder height, pause, and let them drop suddenly to your knees. As you drop your arms, breathe out forcefully. Then say, "Who cares? So what? Svaha!"[3]

Rinpoche's phrases "Who cares?" and "So what?" are more polite versions of Romano's mischievous "Who gives a shit?" They capture the relief of letting go of what we can't control. While sitting retreat, I couldn't control the stories in my head. I could shrug them off, though, and Romano's mantra was an impish reminder to do just that. Tsoknyi Rinpoche's Sanskrit addition of "Svaha!" offers a deeper meaning. *Svaha*, translated as "so be it," takes us beyond letting something go into the more profound and challenging realm of allowing or letting be.

Allowing or letting be is a big topic we have looked at already and will practice throughout this guide. It takes awareness to understand this theme intellectually and to practice it. The promise of meditation is not enlightenment. It's not happiness. It's awareness. The shift in perspective that awareness offers lets us look at the curveballs life throws us as opportunities to practice and provides a set of practical tools to help us deal with them. Curveballs like:

You're in a pitch meeting for work or doing something else that's time-sensitive, and the phone rings. It's a personal call from a family member who needs your help immediately.

Or, when your cell phone rings, you're in the middle of a romantic dinner with your partner or a cozy dinner with your family. It's a work call from a colleague, and a significant project needs your attention now.

You get into a fender bender on your way to a concert, game, play, or to your closest friend from high school's birthday party. You've looked forward to this event for a long time but can't attend because you spend the evening getting your car towed to the repair shop instead.

Our automatic stress response will often kick in when we're caught off guard in situations like these. Awareness can put it in perspective along with the circumstances that triggered it.

"Running away from any problem only increases the distance from the solution" is a popular meme that works as a reminder of why allowing is essential. Our feelings will change if we acknowledge how we feel, relax, and hold on. They may not change exactly how we hope, but something will shift. With patience, we're ready to practice allowing. Allowing is not the same as running away from our problems. Allowing means we soften our hearts and stay steady like a log instead of battling against something outside our control. How? By letting go of the struggle and remembering that nothing lasts forever; this, too, will pass. We allow. We let be. We let go of expectations for a particular outcome. And then, we can better meet what's ahead with attention, balance, compassion, and playfulness.

The short version of Reinhold Niebuhr's Serenity Prayer from Alcoholics Anonymous and Al-Anon describes what allowing looks like in action: "God grant me the serenity to accept what I cannot change, the courage to change what I can, and the wisdom to know the difference." Allowing is not the same as nihilism, where nothing matters so we shrug our shoulders and give up. It's more like svaha—"so be it." We don't give up trying to improve our lives and make the world better. We let go of specific expectations for the outcome to focus on the process in a caring, connected way. An additional stanza to the Serenity Prayer, one that's not as well-known as the first, describes what it takes to "allow" when you navigate life's hard stuff. "Grant me patience for the changes that take time, an appreciation for all that I have, tolerance for those with different struggles, and the strength to get up and try again one day at a time." Given the universality of themes across cultures and traditions, it makes sense that the qualities identified in the Serenity Prayer, with its roots in Christianity, track the Buddhist virtues called the paramitas in Sanskrit or the paramis in Pali—specifically patience, diligence, generosity, and wisdom.

WRAP-UP: Awareness and Allowing

Uncomfortable thoughts, emotions, and sensations tend to be less painful and move through us more quickly when we recognize them, understand they are in flux and dependent on causes and conditions outside our control, and let them be. With awareness, we can recognize what is within our control. With allowing, we can accept what is not. The Serenity Prayer offers a long-standing and practical prescription for striking a balance between allowing and action. In so doing, it beautifully captures the essence of several universal themes we explore in this guide, including patience, discernment, and wisdom.

Practice

Lie on your back on a bed and cover yourself with a sheet or a blanket. Rest your head directly on the mattress or on a pillow, whichever is most comfortable. Let your head sink into the bed. Still lying on your back, let your arms and legs rest naturally by your sides. Feel them sink in. Let your feet fall naturally to their sides and feel them sink into the bed. Relax and feel the weight of your full body drop into the mattress. Rest for a moment. Take a deep breath in and hold it for a few seconds. Exhale, then rest your hands on your stomach and breathe naturally. Lightly focus on the outbreath as your hands move up and down on your belly. Keep resting your hands on your stomach or move them to your sides. Expand your awareness to sense the weight of your whole body against the mattress and feel yourself sink in. Notice the support from the mattress beneath you and the warmth from the sheet or blanket that's covering you. Rest in open awareness for as long as you like. If your mind gets busy or you become restless, bring your attention back to your body and scan it again. Start by feeling the weight of your head sink into the mattress, then move your attention from the back of your head to your shoulders, to your back, to your arms and hands, to your rear, legs, and feet. Rest your hands on your stomach and feel the natural rhythm of your breathing again. Lightly focus on your exhale. Last, expand your awareness to include the sensation of your whole body's weight sinking into the mattress and the feeling of the sheet or blanket covering you. Rest there for as long as you like.

Takeaway

Notice the stories you tell yourself when you're frustrated or upset. Does interrupting them with a lighthearted phrase like "who cares?" or "so what?" make room for playfulness, balance, and compassion?

12

Perfect Action

Relaxed, Minimal Effort and Discernment

Wu wei is perhaps the most mind-bending principle in Taoism, an ancient Chinese philosophy and way of life associated, as I mentioned earlier, with Lao Tzu. It means "without doing, causing, or making." But in practice, wu wei is less about doing nothing than doing things in sync with the situation in which we find ourselves. It's akin to allowing, or svaha. In *The Way of Chuang Tzu*, Thomas Merton calls wu wei *perfect action*:

> It is not mere passivity, but it is action that seems both effortless and spontaneous because performed "rightly" in perfect accordance with our nature and our place in the scheme of things. It is completely free because there is in it no force and no violence. It is not "conditioned" or "limited" by our own individual needs and desires, or even by our own theories and ideas.[1]

I couldn't make sense of wu wei the first time I read about it. The principle sounded good in theory but was far from the path I had followed to be successful. Earlier, I wrote that relaxation did not come to me naturally and that, more often than once, I had worked myself into a state of exhaustion. From childhood, I had been taught that the harder you try, the better the outcome, and I believed it, even though as an adult I knew from experience that it wasn't always true. Growth and effort go hand in hand, but not necessarily the way conventional wisdom would have us think. The quality and amount of effort necessary to get something done matters, and it changes with each situation. Although counterintuitive, it would be more accurate to say that the optimal level of effort is the least required to do what needs to be done, and the optimal type of effort is relaxed.

....

We are going for relaxed, minimal effort.

....

Relaxed, minimal effort is what Aldous Huxley called the law of reversed effort and Alan Watts called the backwards law. I had a Baader-Meinhof moment when I first connected the relaxed, minimal effort embodied by wu wei with its countless examples in daily life. The thought experiment "Don't think about a white bear" is one example, and the principle that battling with our thoughts and emotions is counterproductive is another. When I began to work with this Taoist principle directly, its purposeful application became central to how I teach, write, and navigate the world.

The perfect action of wu wei—the relaxed, minimal effort necessary to get something done—is often compared to water. The water that flows down a river doesn't battle with or try to move the rocks that block its way. It flows with the current, not against it, by washing over and around the rocks. My favorite book on Chinese philosophy, *The Tao of Pooh*, tells a classic story about a man who falls down a waterfall to illustrate wu wei. Onlookers by the side of a great waterfall see an elderly man being tossed back and forth in the churning water. Certain that he will drown, the onlookers rush to the riverbed to rescue him. The man is out of the water and on the bank when they arrive. He's singing! When the onlookers ask him how he was able to survive, the old man replies, "I go down with the water and come up with the water. I follow it and forget myself. I survive because I don't struggle against the water's superior power. That's all."[2]

If you know how to swim, you've practiced wu wei, and if you've taught a child to float, you've explained it. When we float on our backs in the water, we're more likely to sink if we struggle to stay afloat. It's easier to float when we trust that we'll be okay and make minimal effort. Like floating in the water, meditation comes naturally, so long as we stay out of our own way. We can thwart our meditation if we get tense and try too hard. Learning to meditate is a lot like learning to float.

I wondered if the instructions swim teachers use to teach people to float are like meditation instructions. When I typed "how to float" into a search engine, I found several sets of clear, concise instructions that could have as easily been for meditators as for swimmers. I've paraphrased them below in bold. Look at the similarities!

Relaxation and trust are crucial to floating, and that's a significant hurdle for some beginners. When you lie back on the water or sit on a meditation cushion for the first time, it's easy to get scared. Your mind and body might respond to fear or other big feelings by becoming restless or tense. You're sure to sink when you're trying to float if you get agitated and tense. Something similar happens when you meditate. If you struggle against the thoughts, emotions, and sensations that pop up during meditation, it's challenging to find a resting place.

Posture is essential even though you're lying on your back in the water. Imagine there's a piece of string attached to your chest that connects with the sky and lifts you. Meditation instructions also emphasize posture. They encourage meditators to imagine a string attached to the crown of their head that raises them upright to support a relaxed yet alert stance of attention.

It's easier to stay steady and not tilt from side to side when you lightly engage your abdominal muscles. The same is true when you meditate. To stay relaxed and upright, lightly engage your core.

Don't try too hard. Instead, listen to your body. Make minor adjustments if needed. Lie back, relax, and let go. It would be challenging to come up with a better set of instructions for relaxed, minimal effort. Relaxing and letting go are as important when we meditate as when we float.

When learning to float, find a safe spot in shallow water to practice and ask a friend to spot you. New meditators are encouraged to enlist a meditation buddy, too. Having good friends is one of the foundations of spiritual life.

If you start to sink, align your body with the surface of the water and try again. Like the other instructions to float, this one applies equally to meditation. Don't worry if you get lost in thought when you meditate. Consider it an opportunity to begin again.

Floating is not the only real-world example of the backwards law. The more you look at any action through the lens of relaxed, minimal effort, the more you will see the applications of wu wei. When we try to see the bottom of a pond through muddy water, we recognize that the more we splash around in the water, the messier it gets. If we leave the water alone, the mud will settle, and the water will clear. We teach children this lesson using a snow globe, glitter jar, or bowl of water and baking soda. The more we shake the water in the globe, jar, or bowl, the cloudier the water becomes and the harder it is to see through it. But if we leave the water alone, the snow, glitter, or baking soda settle, and children can see through to the other side.

The branch of a weeping willow tree in a snowstorm is another example of wu wei. The hefty branch of a mighty oak tree can break under the weight of heavy snow because it cannot bend. But heavy snow doesn't break a flexible willow branch. When the snow melts or blows off a willow branch, it springs back.

A fly stuck in honey is an unfortunate example of what can happen when we exert too much effort. Flies are drawn to the sweet smell of honey and get stuck when they swoop in to take a closer look. The more the fly struggles to get unstuck, the more trapped it becomes.

In judo and other martial arts, gentleness and pliability are the keys to relaxed, minimal effort. A martial artist dances and parries around their opponent, exhausting them instead of harming them with brute force.

The opposite of relaxed, minimal effort is an internal or external tug-of-war. A common example of an inner tug-of-war is when our thoughts and emotions conflict. "Maybe this, maybe that" is an internal tug-of-war with which I am all too familiar. A classic example of an outer tug-of-war is a power struggle. If you're a parent, I bet you've been in more than one of them:

"Put on your jacket."

"I don't want to put on my jacket."

"It's cold outside; you need a jacket."

"No, I don't."

"Yes, you do,"

"*Noooo*, I don't."

Our kids are not the only people with whom we have power struggles. Any situation where two or more people are meant to row together in the same direction is ripe for one. What would happen if the next time you're in a metaphorical tug-of-war with someone, you drop the rope—if there was nothing for your child, partner, sibling, or coworker to tug against? What would happen if the next time you're in a metaphorical tug-of-war with yourself, you drop the rope—if instead of allowing your thoughts and emotions to battle with each other, you allow them to be in conflict? Dropping the rope is a real-life example of wu wei and when doing nothing is the perfect action.

Don't get me wrong. Sometimes it's not wise to drop the rope, and instead we need to puzzle out a confusing internal conflict or step in and take control of an external one. Suppose your children need to get to school on time and you're running late. If they don't want to get in the car, you might need to scoop them up and buckle them in, even though they are upset and resist. More often than we think, though, the outcome doesn't matter much. These are opportunities to hone our discernment by dropping the rope and watching the dynamic shift. When we drop the rope in an external conflict, our inaction telegraphs to a family member, friend, or coworker we trust that "they've got this." We're signaling to them that we're on the same team and have confidence that they can figure out whether they need a coat, for example, even if it takes weathering the experience of being cold without one.

When we drop the rope in an internal game of tug-of-war, we practice allowing, svaha, or letting be. One of the most important principles in meditation—one that's easy to forget when we're in the thick of it—is to leave our thoughts and feelings alone and allow them to be just as they are. What arises in our minds and bodies is far less important than how we relate to it. It's okay to be with whatever arises, even when what arises is unpleasant. Applying this principle requires us to trust that nothing terrible will happen if we let our thoughts and emotions alone because we have the capacity to stay with the ups and downs of daily life. When we trust in our essential goodness and resilience, we don't need to be reactive.

By recognizing how often we dig in our heels about things that don't matter much, we see how easily we get caught up in stories about what might happen or what other people might think. These are priceless opportunities to look with discernment at the stories we tell ourselves. You can allow a story to run its course if you pause and drop into a moment of awareness. Without paying too much attention to what you think, check how you feel. What's happening in your body and mind? Then, with relaxed, minimal effort, ask yourself, "Is this a moment when I can be more flexible and responsive?" Often, the answer is yes. That's perfect action. We don't drop the rope when the issue we're sparring about is not negotiable. Then, we dig in our heels and respond kindly with relaxed, minimal effort—not emotionally, but compassionately and with discernment. That's perfect action too.

WRAP-UP: Relaxed, Minimal Effort and Discernment

While writing this book, I thought about the universal themes that show up time and again when I teach mindfulness and meditation. Unexpectedly, the theme that came up the most was wu wei. I had long understood its relevance and importance, but it wasn't until I started to write about it that I saw it for the shapeshifter it most certainly is. Wu wei appears in different ways, shapes, and forms in almost every meditation experience I have and mindfulness lesson I teach. Even when I emphasize another theme—everything changes, for instance, or is interdependent—peeking out from behind that theme is a reminder that pushing the idea through to hammer it home is counterproductive. Not trying too hard does not mean giving up on an idea, not working diligently, or not being resolute in purpose. It means that the most effective means to an end involves effort to be sure, but that effort needs to be coupled with flexibility and responsiveness. That's relaxed, minimal effort and discernment.

Practice 1

If you get caught in an internal tug-of-war when you meditate, see what happens if you respond with less effort. Allow your mind to be open and aware without analyzing your thoughts and feelings. There will be plenty of time to think through your problems when you're done meditating. Getting lost in thoughts and emotions is natural, but you don't need to get swept away by them; you can respond with relaxed, minimal effort instead. Notice if your shift in effort and perspective makes a difference.

Takeaway 1

If you are frustrated because something is not going the way you had hoped, lean back rather than leaning in. See what happens if you respond with less effort.

Practice 2

If you are in a power struggle with a colleague or your teenager, if your toddler has a meltdown, or if your boss flips their lid, put some psychic space between the stimulus and your response to see if this shift in your effort, energy, and perspective makes a difference.

Takeaway 2

When you find yourself in an outer tug-of-war, ask yourself whether the argument you're having matters much. Is this the hill you want to die on? If not, drop the rope and look for the ripple effects.

13

What Will You Do in the Bardo?[1]

Openness and Change

As a young boy, Mingyur Rinpoche lived near his father's hermitage, Nagi Gompa, located in the mountains outside of Kathmandu, Nepal. Kathmandu is a busy, loud, and densely populated city. When one of Mingyur Rinpoche's older brothers moved from his quiet mountain life to the noisy urban hubbub Kathmandu, he had a hard time adjusting. As Rinpoche tells the story in his book *In Love with the World*, day and night in the city cars honked, dogs barked, songs blasted from transistor radios, and fake gurus shouted sermons through loudspeakers. When Rinpoche's brother came home to visit, he told his father that he felt stressed and had trouble sleeping due to the noise and commotion. With genuine concern, Tulku Urgyen Rinpoche, considered to be one of the greatest meditation teachers and practitioners of all time, asked his son, "What will you do in the bardo?"

At four months, four years, forty, eighty, and older, we are in the process of evolving. From the most common perspective, the transition from birth to death begins when we're born and ends when we die. Like a snapshot in time, though, every moment in our lives is also a transition. In Tibetan Buddhism, there's a word for life's transitions large and small: *bardo*. Bardo refers to six stages of life-and-death transitions; the first three stages happen when we're alive, the fourth leads up to the moment of death, and the last two are a transition between dying and being reborn. For those who believe in reincarnation, the transitional stages between death and rebirth are what many think of when they hear the word *bardo*. According to the traditional bardo teachings, how we navigate this transition between death and rebirth may determine whether we come back to life as a dung beetle or as royalty.

For me, the jury is out on whether death is the end or if something comes after it. There are no verifiable first-person accounts of what it's like to be in the bardo, at least none that I know of. There are reliable accounts of near-death experiences (NDEs) though, which meditators imagine are like the bardo between death and rebirth. NDEs are triggered by singular life-threatening experiences, when people are under serious threat, severely ill, or close to death. They are not unusual, nor are they fanciful flights of imagination. They are remarkably common (one in ten patients with cardiac arrest in a hospital setting, for example) and, according to an article in *Scientific American*, are probably underreported due to "shame, social stigma, and pressure to conform to the prototype of the 'blissful' near-death experience."[2] Arguably, people tend not to report negative ones because they are contrary to the popular image of NDEs.

From as early as the Middle Ages (and some say ancient times), people have written about NDEs. One of the best-known descriptions is from Ernest Hemingway, who wrote about being critically injured by an exploding shell on a battlefield in World War I. In a letter home, he said:

Dying is a very simple thing. I've looked at death, and really I know. If I should have died it would have been very easy for me. Quite the easiest thing I ever did.³

Researchers have interviewed thousands of people who have had NDEs and can describe them. "Though details and descriptions vary across cultures," writes Gideon Lichfield for *The Atlantic*, "the overall tenor of the experience is remarkably similar.... Many of these stories relate the sensation of floating up and viewing the scene around one's unconscious body...."⁴ This description sounds a lot like what meditators describe as groundlessness, and groundlessness can be disconcerting regardless of where and when it happens.

The classical bardo teachings in Tibetan Buddhism offer a set of practices that give meditators a chance to psychologically prepare for death by imagining what the groundlessness of dying feels like and learning to navigate it. Many find these practices helpful and reassuring. Contemporary teachers in the Tibetan tradition have reimagined classical bardo practices so they can be used to prepare for the feeling of groundlessness that accompanies any life transition, not just death—like a new job, the loss of someone you love, or a shock. In *In Love with the World,* Mingyur Rinpoche connects the dots for us:

[T]he bardo stages then illuminate how these iconic death-to-life transitions emerge in everyday experience.... Without some understanding of the natural transitions, it's easy to get stuck.

He continues:

The bardos show that everything is always in transition. And whether "becoming" applies to transitions between mental identifications within this lifetime or over many lifetimes, the challenge remains the same: to liberate ourselves by letting go of grasping on to our self-constructed narratives.[5]

Periods of transition, growth, and change—both big and small—present us with an opportunity to become comfortable with feeling groundless and to manage uncertainty with attention, balance, compassion, and playfulness. Transitions are, by their very nature, uncertain. We plan, forecast, and prepare for changes ahead; still, aspects of every transition are outside our control. As a result, everyone gets the rug pulled out from under them sometimes. The reimagined bardo teachings are a way to get some practice dealing with feeling groundless before it happens. By giving meditators a road map to become comfortable with uncertainty, the bardo teachings are helpful, practical tools to use throughout life. From this perspective, the question "What will you do in the bardo?" is another way of asking "What will you do when it feels like the rug has been pulled out from under you?" In her book *Living Beautifully: With Uncertainty and Change*, Pema Chödrön describes feeling groundless as "this underlying energy that is so threatening to the part of us that wants certainty."[6] The funny thing about wanting certainty is that if you're reading this guide, I bet you already know it is an illusion. Even when we do our best to understand something, someone, or a situation, it's impossible to know everything that is happening now or that led up to this moment. The truth is there's often more we don't know than we do know. Sometimes we don't have enough information. Sometimes the mysteries of life are too mysterious.

Great thinkers have long recognized the limitations of being certain and the benefits of being open-minded. In a 1936 article for *Esquire* entitled "The Crack-Up," F. Scott Fitzgerald, author of *The Great Gatsby*, wrote his familiar maxim:

> [T]he test of a first-rate intelligence is the ability to hold two opposed ideas in the mind at the same time, and still retain the ability to function. One should, for example, be able to see that things are hopeless and yet be determined to make them otherwise.[7]

Unfortunately, being open-minded doesn't necessarily come easily, nor does the determination to keep going when things feel hopeless. But we can incline our minds in that direction. How? By developing what the poet John Keats described as "negative capability."

In an 1817 letter to his brothers, Keats described a conversation he had with friends while walking home from a Christmas pantomime. The conversation was about the qualities one needs to be a "man of achievement." In Keats's view, the most important quality is:

> [N]egative capability, that is when a man is capable of being in uncertainties, mysteries, doubts, without any irritable reaching after fact and reason.

"[Keats isn't using the word *negative*] in a pejorative sense," writes Stephen Hebron in an article for the British Library, "but to convey the idea that a person's potential can be defined by what he or she does *not* possess." Hebron continues, "Essential to literary achievement, Keats argues, is a certain passivity, a willingness to let what is mysterious or doubtful remain just that."[8] Neither Keats nor Fitzgerald were the first great thinkers to recognize negative capability as a sign of a first-rate intelligence. Socrates came to the same conclusion in the fifth century before the Common Era. In *A History of Western Philosophy*, Bertrand Russell writes,

> The Platonic Socrates consistently maintains that he knows nothing, and is only wiser than others in knowing that he knows nothing; but he does not think knowledge unobtainable. On the contrary, he thinks the search for knowledge of the utmost importance.[9]

Meditation invites openness and intellectual humility as we recognize and accept the limits of human knowledge while we continue to learn and grow. Books, classes, university, and even the school of hard knocks are opportunities to develop our intellect. What meditation offers is different though. Among other things, it gives us a method to let the dust settle in our minds, so we can investigate what's happening within and around us with more clarity. We watch. We feel. We intuit. And we notice that everything is made up of multiple interdependent elements that are ever-changing. The sandcastles we build on the beach wash away when the tide comes in. People are born, and if they're lucky they grow old, and they die. These are examples of multiplicity, change, and interdependence that we see with our own two eyes; what we can see on a gross level. There are also ones that are harder to see. Even if something looks like a solo actor—constant, independent, and staying the same—something is shifting on a subtle level. A duck looks like it's staying still when it floats on the surface of a pond, but we know this appearance is deceiving. Its webbed feet are busy paddling underwater to keep it from drifting; we just can't see them.

Earlier, we compared the vast perspectives of the magnificent Hubble and Webb telescopes to our more limited ones to remind us of the parameters of our all-too-human view. But perhaps a better example of the confines of human perception comes from the natural world—specifically, the many ways that the sensory systems of animals, birds, and insects tune in to aspects of the environment that human sensory systems can't pick up, such as surface vibrations, smells, tastes, light, colors, heat, sounds, echoes, electric fields, and magnetic fields. A quick survey of some of what other species perceive that humans miss entirely is eye-opening.

Sight. A robin or sparrow sees an entire dimension of colors that we cannot see, while bees, using ultraviolet vision, see patterns on flowers that guide them to the flower's pollen—patterns beyond human perception.

Sense. Fish sense currents in a body of water that humans cannot feel. Even in the dark, rattlesnakes sense our presence by picking up heat from our bodies' infrared radiation, while birds navigate in the dark by detecting the earth's magnetic field.

Smell. Our pet dogs and cats have highly developed senses of smell that pick up odors we're oblivious to, and seabirds take in smells rising from a water's surface that we can't detect.

Sound. Our pet dogs and cats also have a keen sense of hearing that picks up sounds we can't make out. Elephants, whales, and other large mammals hear low-frequency sounds that we can't hear without the aid of technology, while bats, dolphins, rodents, and certain insects perceive sounds at higher frequencies than we can detect on our own.

Echolocation. Bats, dolphins, and other marine animals and bird species use an extraordinary sensory mechanism called echolocation to perceive and interact with their surroundings. These species communicate, locate prey, navigate diverse and complex surroundings, and survive predators by emitting sound waves, then listening to the echoes that bounce back off objects in their environments.

In his remarkable book *An Immense World: How Animal Senses Reveal the Hidden Realms around Us*, Pulitzer Prize–winning science writer Ed Yong explains that every animal (including us) lives within a sensory bubble that limits how it understands the world. He suggests that this is "a call for humility." Our sensory environment is "all that we know," writes Yong, "and so we easily mistake it for all there is to know." He elaborates,

> [F]or all our vaunted intelligence, it is very hard for us to understand other creatures, or to resist the tendency to view their senses through our own. We can study the physics of an animal's environment, look at what they respond to or ignore, and trace the web of neurons that connects their sense organs to their brains. But the ultimate feats of understanding—working out what it's like to be a bat, or an elephant, or a spider—always require what psychologist Alexandra Horowitz calls "an informed imaginative leap."[10]

Quantum theory is way over my head, but it is another area of scientific exploration that calls for intellectual humility. Like centuries of contemplatives before them, quantum researchers and theorists tell us that everything is made up of multiple changing and interdependent elements, and there are limits to what we can know. Don't take my word for it; take the word of Jonny Thomson, who teaches philosophy at Oxford University and posted this on Instagram (the emphasis in bold was added by me):

> For a lot of people, quantum might as well mean "magic." It's a subatomic universe of photons "wanting" to do things and waves deciding to behave like particles, and everyone pretends that makes sense. According to the Copenhagen Interpretation (yes, even quantum physicists can't agree about quantum physics), there are three principles to the quantum world:
>
> First, quantum objects **will change** depending on if and how they are observed . . .
>
> The second principle is that **nothing in nature is fixed, but a probability** . . .
>
> The final principle is that **we can never know all the values of a system at the same time** . . .[11]

Even though we know better, it is tempting to oversimplify our thoughts, emotions, sensations, and beliefs. We tend to put them in neat compartments of good and bad, right and wrong, black and white. Allowing ourselves to accept uncertainty and the discomfort that comes with it, rather than compartmentalize, helps meditators develop a mindset that is far broader than the one that's prevalent in much of our achievement-oriented culture—a shift in perspective that has remarkably concrete and helpful applications. A more open and less linear mindset supports the development of the negative capability Keats wrote about, one that's okay with experiences being difficult or complex. It lessens one's need to solve problems immediately, freeing up more mental bandwidth to recognize the nuances in a situation and respond without a set agenda but with thoughtfulness and curiosity instead. Through this lens, a challenging experience often turns out to be a positive turning point that leads to a richer, more complex, and more fulfilling life.

WRAP-UP:
Openness and Change

The nature of mind and most everything else is subtle, interdependent, and always changing—too rich and complex for snap judgments. Even when we do our best to understand something and look at it from every angle, we don't always have the information we need to make an informed decision. Still, uncertainty can make us uncomfortable, and it's tempting to jump to conclusions and oversimplify what we see. Then, we might make a decision too quickly, before we have enough information. What if we allow ourselves to relax and be okay with not knowing? While it might be uncomfortable not to have a ready-made answer, uncertainty is okay. In the space of not knowing, an explanation often emerges, and if it doesn't, we gain confidence in our ability to navigate uncertainty and change. We might even become so comfortable that we can respond to uncertainty by saying "I don't know" or "I don't know yet, but I'm curious to find out."

Practice

Find a comfortable place to sit outside or near a window. Relax and close your eyes. Take a deep breath, hold it for a moment, then exhale. Breathe naturally with a light emphasis on the outbreath. When you're ready and with your eyes closed, listen to the sounds around you.

Choose one sound and listen to it closely. If you're someplace quiet, listen to the absence of sound. If silence is something you can hear, is it a sound? Where did the sound, or the sound of silence, come from? Can you track it back to its very beginning? Stay with the sound until it changes or fades away. Why did it change? Where did it go?

Let go of these questions and allow your mind to be open without focusing on a specific object. Now, you're practicing open awareness. Rest here for a few moments.

When you're ready, open your eyes and softly rest your gaze ahead of you without focusing on a specific object. What's changing in your field of vision? The light might change, traffic may move, or you might see that the wind is blowing. What do you know about what you're seeing? What don't you know? Choose one object and softly focus on it. Where did it come from? How did it get here? If it's changing, why is it changing? Dig deeper and look for subtler changes than the ones you see.

Let go of these inquiries and allow your mind to be open and aware. Continue practicing open awareness for as long as you like.

Takeaway

Can you embrace uncertainty by letting your thoughts and emotions be? If discomfort comes with uncertainty, can you allow yourself to experience it? Remember, we can never be certain what will happen next because nothing exists on its own—everything is made up of multiple parts and pieces that are interdependent and changing.

14

The Stories We Tell Ourselves

Awareness and Investigation

Los Angeles comedian/podcaster Marc Maron tells this story at Largo, an iconic comedy club in West Hollywood. Maron is getting into his car in a Whole Foods parking lot, and a second driver is waiting for him to pull out of the space. A third car pulls up. Not seeing what is going on, the driver of the third car honks at the comic. Maron informs him that another car is already waiting. In response, the honker shouts an obscenity and makes a rude gesture. Maron could escalate the situation but instead he jokingly says, "Atta boy." The honker speeds off, but not without comment. Out the window as he drives from the lot, he shouts, "P#*@y"—a vulgar word that means coward or weakling. Maron proceeds to second-guess his own low-key response for the rest of his act.

Los Angeles with its rush hour and congested traffic has plenty of road rage, where drivers react to a perceived slight aggressively and without thinking. The stimulus and response seem to emerge simultaneously, but they don't—a phenomenon that is described in this well-worn maxim that's often misattributed to Viktor Frankl:

Between stimulus and response there is a space. In that space is our power to choose our response. In our response lies our growth and our freedom.[1]

Managing hecklers from the stage of a comedy club for decades (and there was one at Largo the night Maron did this bit) likely honed Maron's skill to choose his rejoinder rather than respond automatically. Meditation is a more accessible way to develop this skill. Through careful investigation, we can tease apart three aspects of perception—awareness, direct experience, and add-ons—to find the space between stimulus and response.

Awareness

Awareness is always with us, but here's the rub: we don't always recognize it and, even when we do, it can be hard to maintain that recognition. Absent awareness, we naturally default to habituated ways of thinking, doing, and seeing. Then it's easy for our perspectives to get skewed—we jump to conclusions, lose sight of what's good in our lives, and get stuck mulling over what's bothering us. Going about our business without awareness is like flying a plane on autopilot. Some familiar tasks are more quickly and accurately executed without conscious thought. This is when the automatic mode is the safest and most efficient way to get things done.[2] Autopilot is not the best approach when confronted with new information, though, especially in an unfamiliar situation. Then we need to tap into our natural awareness. Awareness can feel quite ordinary and simple, like when we're mindful of the sounds in a room, and there are times that awareness comes as an extraordinary flash of insight.

....

Meditation builds our capacity to
recognize awareness and stay with it.

....

Like the terms *enlightenment* and *the Tao* that we previously considered, awareness is better understood as an experience than an idea. It might be best explained by, "You'll know it when you see it," or better yet, "You'll know it when you experience it." That's why it's helpful when someone points it out to you. The most straightforward way I've seen awareness explained is by Mingyur Rinpoche, who leads a series of activities that allow new meditators to experience awareness before they try to understand it conceptually. I have watched Mingyur Rinpoche lead this activity many times, but the specific example I offer below is from a video he recorded for Tergar International's parent program:

Please raise your hand.
Do you know you're raising your hand?
Awareness is knowing you are raising your hand.

Rub the palms of your hands together for a few moments
   and then stop.
Do you know you're rubbing your palms together?
Awareness is knowing you are rubbing your palms together.

How do your hands feel? Are they warm? Smooth?
   Rough?
Do you know your hands feel warm, smooth, or rough?
Awareness is knowing your hands feel warm, smooth, or rough.

Hold the palms of your hands apart, so they're not
   touching.
Do you feel any sensations? Not many, right?
What about awareness, is it still here?
Awareness is knowing that you're not feeling many
   sensations.

Now, clap your hands together.
Do your palms sting or burn? Probably, right?
Where's awareness now?
Awareness is knowing your palms are stinging or burning.

Mingyur Rinpoche's activity-based instruction on awareness
might seem like nothing special at first glance, but its simplicity
is deceiving.

Direct Experience

Let's look at the activity again. This time, we'll focus on the direct
experience: what a friendly and impartial observer would say
happened. Now that we've found awareness, where's the direct
experience?

Please raise your hand.
The direct experience is raising your hand.

Rub the palms of your hands together for a few moments
   and then stop.
The direct experience is rubbing your palms together.

How do your hands feel? Are they warm? Smooth?
Rough?
*The direct experience is the sensation of warmth, smoothness,
or roughness.*

Hold the palms of your hands apart, so they're not
touching.
Do you feel any sensations now? Not many, right?
*The direct experience is feeling the absence of many
sensations.*

Now, clap your hands together.
Do the palms of your hands sting or burn? Probably, right?
*The direct experience is the stinging or burning in the palms
of your hands.*

Add-Ons

Add-ons are the thoughts, opinions, and beliefs we have about
an experience.[3] We found awareness and the direct experience are
there any add-ons?

Imagine that you think this exercise is silly, but you raise
your hand anyway.
What's the direct experience?
The direct experience is raising your hand.

What is thinking the exercise is silly?
The add-on is thinking that raising your hand is silly.

Where is awareness?
*Awareness is knowing that you are raising your hand and
that you think it's silly.*

Awareness gives us an opportunity to tease apart the *direct experience* (what's happening) and what we *add on to it* (our analysis, judgments, and stories about what's happening). Two final examples:

Imagine that you are doing this activity with colleagues
and feel self-conscious. .

What is the direct experience?
*There are two direct experiences: doing the activity and
feeling self-conscious.*

Where is awareness?
*Awareness is knowing you are doing the activity and feeling
self-conscious.*

Imagine that the following pops into your mind as you do the activity: "My colleagues think these exercises are silly and will judge me harshly for wasting their time."

What is the direct experience?
The direct experience is doing the activity.

What is the add-on?
The add-on is the story you tell yourself.

Where is awareness?
*Awareness is knowing that you are doing the activity and
telling yourself a story.*

There can be more than one direct experience at a time. The
thoughts and emotions that bubble up in response to an experience are also a second experience; they are not always an add-on.
In the example above, doing the activity is one direct experience
and feeling self-conscious is another. To keep this simple, I'm
focusing on each as a direct experience. But, without going too far
down this rabbit hole, feeling self-conscious is both an add-on to
the first direct experience—doing the activity—and a direct experience of the emotions that underlie being self-conscious. There
can be layers and layers of direct experiences and add-ons. The
point is not to get the add-ons to stop, but to stay with awareness. Then we can distinguish between the direct experience and
what we add to it. The add-ons will ease on their own eventually if,
instead of getting lost in thought by analyzing them, we stay with
awareness. The layers of analysis, judgment, and storytelling that
we bring to an experience are different from the direct emotional
experience of feeling self-conscious. The emotions that fuel our
self-consciousness don't need to be a problem. It's the stories we
tell ourselves about why we're self-conscious that can become one.

Review

Awareness is the key to finding the growth and freedom promised
in the quote at the beginning of this chapter often misattributed to
Frankl. To see the space between stimulus and response we must

identify the direct experience and tease it apart from the stories we add to it. That takes awareness. To recap:

Is raising your hand awareness?
What about *knowing* you're raising your hand?

When you rub your hands together, is that awareness?
What about *knowing* that you're rubbing your hands together?

Is the tingling or burning in your hands after you clap them awareness?
What about *knowing* your palms tingle or burn after you clap your hands?

Is feeling self-conscious when you do these exercises awareness?
What about *knowing* you feel self-conscious?

Is it awareness when you speculate on what other people think?
What about *knowing* that you're speculating?

Remarkably, we often treat add-ons as if they are real even though they are not. The thought of a sweater is not the same as the actual sweater, right? The sweater has substance—color, weight, and form. The thought of a sweater has no more substance than a reflection in a mirror. If thoughts and emotions have no substance, why do we give them so much attention? In real life and real time the direct experience and what we add to it can be so tightly entangled that they seem like the same "thing," and that "thing" feels real. When we use awareness to tease apart the add-on from the direct experience, we are better able to see our thoughts, emotions, and beliefs for what they are—dreamlike, with no more substance than the reflection in a mirror.

Real-World Applications

Investigating anything through layers of thoughts, opinions, and stories is like looking at a reflection in a foggy mirror. The fog that clouds the reflection can also distort the image. In contrast, using awareness to distinguish direct experience from add-ons is like looking at our mind's activity in a clean mirror. It's natural to have judgments, opinions, and stories about what we experience, but they don't need to fog our vision. Instead of getting lost in the fog, a clear mirror of awareness allows us to investigate what's happening inside and out with playfulness, attention, balance, and compassion.

To teach this skill in mindfulness lessons, I use an activity I learned while taking childbirth classes over thirty years ago, where expectant mothers practiced pain management strategies like deep breathing while holding a melting ice cube in their hands. In mindfulness, we use this activity to investigate the direct experience of holding a cube of melting ice and our reactions to that experience.

The sensation of the ice melting in your hand is the first direct experience that we explore. Your mindfulness practice is to investigate the sensations you feel with clear mirrorlike awareness—even if they are unpleasant—and notice their interdependent and changing nature.

If you shift focus from sensations to thoughts and emotions, you can investigate the add-ons—your mental reactions to holding the melting ice—with clear mirror-like awareness. These add-ons are the thoughts, emotions, and stories you tell yourself about the activity. You might think, "It's cold, my hands sting, and I can't hold the ice much longer!" Or "Look at me, I can hold this ice easily even though it stings a bit!" The content of what you're thinking doesn't matter. What matters is that you recognize the difference between the direct experience you're investigating (what it feels like to hold the ice) and the add-ons (what you tell yourself about it).

You could also let your mind be open and not focus on anything particular. Then, with clear mirror-like open awareness, you can investigate the full range of your experience—the sensations, stories, and feelings that emerge while holding a melting ice cube, or their absence.

One of my top informal practices is distinguishing between an experience and my mental reactions to it. It's remarkable how placing what's happening into this broader context can stop a negative spiral of thoughts and emotions before it begins. When something feels off and emotionally charged, I ask myself to identify the aspects of the experience that objectively happened and separate them from the stories I tell myself. Here's an example.

It's not my best quality, but I am overly protective of family members and friends. If someone or something hurts one of them, it takes a herculean effort on my part not to try and rescue them. Recently, my husband dealt with a challenging work experience and so did each of my adult children. It didn't matter how much I knew about their work or the people on the other side of their challenging experiences, I had plenty of opinions. I had opinions about the other peoples' motivations, their levels of talent, their skillfulness, and what they should or shouldn't have done. You name it and I had an opinion about it. Decades of meditation have taught me that trying to stop my opinions from bubbling up is ineffective at best and counterproductive at worst. Remember social psychologist Dan Wegner's thought experiment "Don't think about a white bear"? I wasn't going to make that mistake. Even though there was not much I could do about whether my overly protective instincts would pop up, I could choose how to relate to them when they did. By identifying aspects of the situations that could be verified and separating them from the stories I told myself, I pulled the rug out from under the negative spiral that was poised in the background and ready to take off. I also gleaned valuable insights into my family members' mindsets and my own.

I do my best to remember this practice when I feel upset. When someone crosses a loved one, it can trigger an intense emotional reaction. More often, though, my triggers are subtler. When a friend or colleague doesn't respond to one of my texts or emails, for instance, the stories I tell myself are laughable. The unresponsive correspondent is "ghosting me," I might say to myself. I might also think, "They're angry," or maybe, "Something's wrong and they are hurt." These are just a few of the inaccurate, fanciful stories I have told myself. Here, it's easy to separate out what can be objectively verified (they didn't answer my email yet) and my stories (everything else). Other situations can be harder, like if you're sick and waiting for the results of medical tests. Is your racing heart rate anxiety, or is it indicative of a serious cardiac problem? Or a loved one may be at the site of an environmental disaster (think earthquake, fire, hurricane) and you can't contact them. Is it because they are hurt or that they don't have access to a working phone or computer? It's helpful to practice separating the objective aspects of an experience from conjecture in situations that are not high stakes because it makes separating them in extreme situations more doable.

We don't need to be meditators to do this informal practice, but formal meditation can deepen it. Formal meditation is often compared to physical workouts. (I don't love this analogy, but it gets the idea across.) As exercise builds our physical endurance and capacity, meditation builds our capacity to recognize awareness and stay with it. When our awareness ripens, so does our capacity to recognize subtle emotional reactions and investigate them with a clear eye. I've seen firsthand how formal meditation builds the capacity to recognize and stay with awareness. For that, I owe a debt of gratitude to my teachers and to the tradition in which I was trained.

WRAP-UP: Awareness and Investigation

Awareness recognizes what's here without getting tangled up in the layers of add-ons that inevitably pop up. It's that simple. Our perspectives can get clouded when what we see, hear, and feel (our direct experience) commingle with our opinions, assumptions, and stories about what we see, hear, and feel (our add-ons). It's like looking in a mirror that is so foggy you can't tell the difference between the people and the objects in the background. With awareness we can see what's happening clearly, like when we look at a reflection in a clean mirror and can easily distinguish between the people and the background. Then, with mirrorlike awareness, we can investigate how the experience makes us feel along with our opinions and stories about it. There are many times when this skill is helpful, like when we're frustrated and snap at other people even if we're not sure why we're frustrated or when our emotions are intense and drag us down.

Formal Practice

Close your eyes and settle into the rhythm of your breathing. When you breathe in, know you're breathing in. When you breathe out, know you're breathing out. Breathe naturally and know you're breathing. Thoughts and emotions will come and go. You don't need to block them. You don't need to analyze them. Being aware of them is enough. Notice them, but focus on the sensation of breathing. Do you know that you are breathing in and out? That's awareness. Do you know thoughts and emotions are bubbling up? That's awareness, too. Continue resting in the present moment with open awareness for as long as you'd like.

Informal Practice

When your mind races into the future, come back to the present moment. When you fold your laundry, know that you are folding laundry. Feel how warm the clothes are when you take them out of the dryer. When you smooth out the wrinkles in your shirt, notice how the color and texture change. When your mind moves from folding clothes to something else, gently bring it back to the task at hand. Do the same when you wash dishes, drive to work, comb your child's hair, or brush your teeth. Just do what you're doing and know you're doing it.

Takeaway

When something feels off or emotionally charged, ask yourself what a friendly and impartial spectator would say happened and separate the aspects of the experience that can be verified objectively from the stories you tell yourself. Distinguishing objective aspects of an experience from conjecture leads to greater clarity and understanding.

15

We're Wrong about Everything

Humility and Wisdom

Like many days when I was focused on writing this book, I got up early, wrote in the morning, ate a late lunch, took a walk, then settled in for a nap. But this particular day, I was too wound up to fall asleep easily. The fifth season of *The Crown*, a historical drama about the reign of Queen Elizabeth II, had been recently released on Netflix and I was halfway through it. Watching television or listening to novels that I've already read usually eases me to sleep, so I got the pillow from my bed, grabbed one of my favorite warm woolen throws from the Pendleton National Park series, and cued up episode five—where Princess Diana nearly gets into a car crash because an aggressive, camera-toting carful of fans recognized her while she was stopped at a red light. When the light turned green, she sped away from them and nearly lost control of her car.[1] Something about the pace, the music, and the subject matter upset me. Mildly agitated, I turned off the television and fell asleep on the couch.

I dream when I nap sometimes, and this was one of those times. Perhaps because what I had been watching before I fell asleep was disturbing, my dreams were disturbing too. It was eerie how real they seemed. Well into my rest, something upsetting in my dream woke me up. I reminded myself that the dream wasn't real and fell back asleep, until it woke me again. Once more, I needed to talk myself out of believing that my dream was real. This happened a couple more times until I forced myself to get up from the couch, put on a heavy down jacket, and head out for coffee. Walking in Brooklyn bundled up for the cold weather and now wide awake, it still felt like my dream was real. I was a little disoriented as I walked the few blocks from our apartment to a coffee shop. I ordered a latte and a chocolate chip cookie, hoping the combination of caffeine and sugar would shake me out of it, or at least make me feel better, and they did. Walking back to the apartment, I wondered why this dream was so convincing, especially since every objective consideration of its subject matter underscored the fact that it could not be true. It's easy to forget that the stories we tell ourselves when we're awake are empty, with no substance, just like my dream.

In the last chapter, we compared awareness to a clean mirror, one where we have an unobstructed view of the activity in our minds. We distinguished between a direct experience and our mental reactions to one. We saw that recognizing multiple layers of experience is a useful tool to better understand ourselves. In related chapters, we looked at two approaches for navigating overly busy minds and big feelings:

> Anchor your attention in the present on a neutral or pleasant object (breath, sound, slogan, or a mental image).
> Do nothing to interfere with the activity of your mind by practicing open awareness.

Here, we'll look at a third approach, where we view our minds' activity as empty, like a dream or the reflection in a mirror. This may sound like a big leap. But the root of many of our problems is that we relate to thoughts, emotions, and the stories we tell ourselves as if they're true. If we look right through them to recognize they have no real substance, we can relate to them the way we relate to our dreams. They provide useful information, but that doesn't mean they are true.

In the introduction, I took a stab at demystifying enlightenment by focusing on the experience of enlightenment instead of the concept. Enlightenment is also a concept, though, one with multiple levels that Buddhist scholars have defined in various ways, one of which is the uprooting of attachment, aggression, and ignorance—three mental attitudes (called the three poisons) that are the root of our problems. It's these three poisons that keep us on the hedonic treadmill chasing after what we want and running away from what we don't want. At the heart of the three poisons are ego and survival. Neither ego, survival, nor the three poisons are objectionable when they function in a healthy way; they only become a problem when they don't.

Attachment (sometimes called greed, craving, or desire) is when we pull what we want toward us by accentuating its positive qualities and ignoring its negative ones. (Not to be confused with the emotional bond that's also called attachment which forms in a warm, generous relationship between a parent and child, romantic partners, siblings, friends, and even with a pet.)
Aggression (sometimes called hatred or anger) is when we push away what we think will harm or threaten us by accentuating its negative qualities and ignoring its positive ones.

Ignorance (sometimes called delusion or indifference) is when we close ourselves off from the nature of reality and our own goodness by ignoring the countless and changing ways we connect with and depend on one another. At root, the delusion of the third poison is the mistaken belief that we are solo actors.

The egocentric nature of the three poisons leads us to identify with them, thus reinforcing the common and deeply held belief that we are central to what's happening now, whatever that might be, as in the George Saunders reference from earlier where he jokes about our mistaken belief that we are the center of the universe—the main character in a movie that's written for and about us. When we recognize the changing and interdependent elements that make up our attachment to, aggression toward, or ignorance of something or someone, we more easily see that nobody, absolutely nobody, is the central character in their own movie because no one, absolutely no one, is a single unified self. Why does this matter? Remembering that nothing is a single unified thing helps us get unstuck when we're intellectually or emotionally fixated on something. Getting stuck on a particular outcome or idea makes no sense since all things connect, nothing lasts forever, and everything is made up of multiple elements that are changing.

What's it like when the three poisons are entirely uprooted? That's a tall order. You don't need to be the Buddha to recognize that the three poisons, and the idea of a permanent self that they perpetuate, are dreamlike and empty of inherent existence, though. My ungenerous attachment, aggression, and ignorance are about me, but they aren't who I really am. Your three poisons aren't who you are either. The interconnected bits and pieces that make up our mental attitudes ebb, flow, and change. None of it can be pinned down, but there are a few constants that we can ascribe to these three poisons:

> They are empty and without substance—like the reflection in a mirror.
> They are dependent on countless causes and conditions, some of which we know and some of which we don't know.
> The way we experience them is always changing. There's nothing there, but still we experience something, and it is in flux.

This might not sound like a big revelation. Intellectually, people easily understand that mental attitudes are without substance, interdependent, and always changing, but often they don't act like it. Internalizing this intellectual understanding leads to a visceral, embodied connection with something beyond self-centered desires quite naturally. This is the experience we first looked at in the introduction that the mystics describe as oneness, where the boundaries of our individual identities dissolve and what remains is a profound sense of unity with everything and everyone. When we better understand perception, we can bring a sense of oneness into every day, and we no longer need to have the starring role in a movie called *Me.*

Let's consider the provocative premise offered by Mark Manson in his bestselling book with an equally provocative title, *The Subtle Art of Not Giving a F*ck: A Counterintuitive Approach to Living a Good Life*:

You're wrong about everything (but so am I).[2]

What an outrageous statement! How could it be? But there's some truth here. To conserve energy, our brains act as prediction machines.[3] They navigate our current situation by predicting what will happen next based on personal experience, memories, and information from our sensory channels. Brains are like the auto-complete feature on a phone or search engine; they try to guess the next word in a conversation or a book while we're having the conversation or reading the book. Given that the only data our brains have to work with is the information that comes in through our senses plus our prior knowledge of the world, it's no wonder we're often wrong. What do we do about the limited and biased prediction machines we call our brains? We appreciate them, respect them, and treat them with kindness.

From the perspective of Tibetan Buddhism, everything we experience is the product of our minds. In his important book on the nature of mind called *Revelations of Mind,* Tarthang Tulku, a Tibetan teacher in the Nyingma tradition, writes:

> There is nothing in our experience that does not arise from mind, depend upon, and bear the imprint of mind.[4]

Our perceptions are based on an astoundingly comprehensive system of mental operations that involve our brains, sensory data, personal experience, memories, and labels that are unique to us. In the background right now, our minds are scanning our inner worlds as well as the information about the outer world that we're taking in through our senses. Our minds identify the information and place it into tailor-made categories using a highly complex and individualized set of mental labels they have been creating all our life, usually outside of our awareness. Our minds then interpret the information, put it into context, and our emotions follow. The result?

....

What it's like to be you or me at that moment.

....

This wildly sophisticated system of mental operations and labeling is an iterative process. That's why what it's like to be you and what it's like to be me changes as we learn and grow. Our understanding of the world and ourselves deepens through study and experience. Yet, our labeling system will always be relative because it is custom-made for us based on life experience, how our brains work, and how our bodies work. The same is true for everyone. How I see my car is a product of my mind; how you see it is a product of your mind. The same holds true for my hat, my reputation, and my family relationships. The red cup we both see sitting on a brown dining room table is a product of my mind and yours. That doesn't mean that these things don't exist independent of us, but rather that the way we see them will always be somewhat different from the way anyone else sees them. As we learn and grow, our understanding of the nature of our minds and everything else evolves, along with how we see that same red cup on that same brown dining table. These are some of the reasons it's fair to say there is no such thing as a fully objective perspective. All is relative.

David J. Linden eloquently unpacks this idea in his haunting essay for *The Atlantic,* "A Neuroscientist Prepares for Death: Lessons My Terminal Cancer Has Taught Me about the Mind":

The deep truth of being human is that there is no objective experience. Our brains are not built to measure the absolute value of anything. All that we perceive and feel is colored by expectation, comparison, and circumstance. There is no pure sensation, only inference based on sensation. Thirty minutes fly by in a conversation with a good friend but seem interminable when waiting in line at the DMV. That fat raise you got at work seems nice until you learn that your coworker got one twice as large as yours. A caress from your sweetheart during a loving, connected time feels warm and delightful, but the very same touch delivered during the middle of a heated argument feels annoying and presumptuous, bordering on violation.[5]

When we recognize that there is no objective experience, what's left other than to accept and appreciate how little we know? How can anyone be so sure of themselves that they shut out new possibilities and shrug off other perspectives? But that's what we do sometimes, especially when we're scared and our mind's capacity to solve problems has narrowed. Eventually—if not right away—having a closed mind will backfire, and the more we double down on certainty, the more uncertain and insecure we become. This is another example of wu wei, also known as the law of reversed effort and the backwards law. Consider the preface of Alan Watts's book, *The Wisdom of Insecurity*:

This book, however, is in the spirit of the Chinese sage Lao Tzu, that master of the law of reversed effort, who declared that those who justify themselves do not convince, that to know truth one must get rid of knowledge, and that

nothing is more powerful and creative than emptiness—
from which men shrink.[6]

By acknowledging the limitations of our all-too-human minds,
Lao Tzu connects wu wei to intellectual humility. It makes sense
to meet conflict with flexibility and responsiveness when we recognize that our understanding is limited by what we can perceive
and how we contextualize it. When we become more comfortable
with uncertainty, it's easier to engage in a rich exploration of the
nature of mind and reality with an open mind. The deeper we look
at the nature of our hearts, minds, and the real world, the more
we see that the hold the three poisons have on us is silly. Still, they
create and exacerbate suffering for everyone. Whether it's possible
to uproot the three poisons entirely is an open question. But if we
recognize they have no more substance than a mirror's reflection,
the grip that ungenerous attachment, aggression, and ignorance
have on us will ease.

Even if we can't uproot the three poisons entirely, we can
incline our minds and hearts toward becoming the person we
want to become by skillfully choosing where to place our energy.
The parable of "The Two Wolves" emphasizes the importance of
becoming aware of these choices, especially the thoughts and emotions we reinforce (perhaps unintentionally) through repetition.

I first heard this story from an insightful Lyft driver who
picked me up from Mary Free Bed Rehabilitation Hospital in
Grand Rapids, Michigan. My sister was a patient, recovering from
extensive back surgery, and I was visiting her. I didn't recognize the
driver, but she recognized me from a similar late-night ride from
the rehab center back to my hotel earlier in the week. The driver
asked how my sister was doing and told me she was praying for

her to have a full and quick recovery. I was surprised the driver remembered us and remarked that holding people in mind like she had held us in mind is a quality worth celebrating. She told me she wished her parents and grandparents felt that way. The driver's family thought she was too "woo-woo" and that she needed to toughen up and be more practical. But she disagreed; she told me her philosophy of life was based on the parable of the two wolves.

Long ago, in the heart of the Cherokee Nation, a wise elder and his young grandson walked in friendly silence through the dense woods and up a mountain trail. In a clearing on the heights of an Appalachian peak, the young boy asked a question that had been gnawing at him: "Why is there so much pain and conflict in the world? Why do some people help each other while others hurt one another?"

The grandfather, a respected elder revered for his brave heart and depth of insight, gazed out at the horizon and said, "Inside every person there is a battle raging. It's as if there are two wolves living within us. They are always at odds, vying for control. One wolf is born of fear and feeds on anger, jealousy, and despair. When the fearful wolf takes control, he spreads misery, misunderstanding, and sorrow."

The boy was visibly upset by this idea and asked his grandfather how to make sure the wolf born of fear doesn't wreak havoc. "Because the other wolf," the grandfather said, "is filled with love, hope, and compassion. When the loving wolf prevails, harmony, understanding, and peace follow in his wake, and the world finds meaning."

After a moment the boy asked his grandfather, "Which wolf will win?"

The old Cherokee chief replied, "The one you feed."[7]

By holding in mind two strangers and wishing them well, the warm-hearted Lyft driver fed the best parts of herself. Her caring, kindness, compassion, and agendaless love had a ripple effect that reached me, my sister, my brother-in-law whom I told the next day, and even further to the people we've told since—and perhaps beyond.

WRAP-UP: Humility and Wisdom

Not all the causes and conditions that contribute to growth and evolution are within our control. Some are genetic, others environmental, some pure luck. Still others are a mystery. Knowing this, it makes sense that we can't always control outcomes. That's humility. There is quite a bit about processes that we can control, though. We can choose how we would like to evolve and grow. That's wisdom. To underscore this point, the late Rabbi Zalman Schachter-Shalomi, who participated in a series of historic interfaith dialogues with His Holiness the Fourteenth Dalai Lama in 1990, compared our minds to tofu. From Schachter-Shalomi: "The mind is like tofu. By itself, it has no taste. Everything depends on the flavor of the marinade it steeps in."[8] In other words, we incline our hearts and minds in the direction of what we think, say, and do.

Practice

You have probably experienced the ways that positive and stressful energy differ. Positive energy cheers people up and lightens their load. Stressful energy leaves people mentally and physically exhausted. Both are contagious. Let's imagine for a moment that engineers have developed a power-generating treadmill that uses human energy to generate positive energy. Everyone on the planet has one, and all the treadmills are connected to a single electrical grid. Now, picture everyone running on their personal treadmill at the same time. The amount of clean, renewable positive energy we could create if we all ran together is boundless. Let's think of the converse: the amount of stressful energy that's created when everyone is running on their hedonic treadmills, mindlessly chasing after what they want and away from what they don't want. When we imagine the amount of suffering they create for themselves and others, we get a sense of the "size of the cloth," to borrow again from Naomi Shihab Nye's poem "Kindness." Then, borrowing another line from the poem's final stanza this time, "it is only kindness that makes sense anymore."[9] Kindness toward everyone who navigates their lives with limited and biased perception—that means everyone on the planet, including us. When we truly grok this view, we create an internal environment where humility and compassion emerge naturally.

Takeaway

Reflect on how you would like to evolve and grow. Then, consider what personal qualities it would take to do so and incline what you think, say, and do in their direction.

16

Nobody Is Running the Show— The Habits Chapter

Awareness and Kindness

If everything we experience is the product of our minds, then what or who is directing the mind that creates our experiences? Is there a "me" behind the scenes, or is there something more mysterious going on? I'm not one to count mystery out entirely, but over the past hundred years, researchers from a variety of fields— neurologists, psychologists, geneticists, and sociologists—point to neurological patterns or habits as the driver of over 40 percent of what we think, say, and do. Here is the technical definition of a habit, from Charles Duhigg, author of *The Power of Habit*:

> [T]he choices that all of us deliberately make at some point, and then stop thinking about but continue doing, often every day.[1]

Habits or patterns are like shortcuts; they're basic behaviors we automatically engage in as a response to familiar situations. They come to us easily and rapidly because we've relied on them so often. Helpful habits free up mental and physical resources so we can learn new things and navigate unfamiliar situations. The more we respond to a familiar experience in the same way, the stronger and more automatic the habit becomes. Like everything else, each habit is made up of multiple interrelated and changing elements— physical, emotional, and behavioral. In this chapter, I sometimes distinguish behavioral habits from emotional patterns, even though both have elements of behavior and emotion embedded in them. When behavioral habits and emotional patterns align with our priorities, the less we think about them the better. Our habits are problematic when they lead us away from the life we want to live and the person we want to be.[2]

In laboratory studies worldwide, scientists have learned what it takes to make, change, or break a habit. A habit is a reward-based process triggered by a cue in our environment. Often called a habit loop, the process goes like this: cue, routine, reward. What happens between the cue and routine that causes us to act? It's dopamine, the biological signature of pleasure-seeking and satisfaction. Dopamine is a chemical messenger or neurotransmitter that our brains release under various circumstances, the best known of which is when we feel and anticipate pleasure. Dopamine flips a neurological switch like the autopilot mode on an airplane we discussed earlier to set in motion an automatic mental, physical, and emotional routine. It is strongly associated with desire, ungenerous attachment, and the hedonic treadmill. In a 2017 article in *Scientific American*, Maia Szalavitz elaborates:

[Dopamine could] account for the so-called hedonic treadmill, the sadly universal experience in which what initially makes us ache with desire, over time becomes less alluring, requiring a greater intensity of experience, new degree of novelty, or higher dose to achieve the same joy. (You buy a new car, but driving it soon becomes routine and you start to crave a fancier one.)[3]

If you use Facebook, Twitter, LinkedIn, Instagram, or TikTok, you've seen a dark side of dopamine where otherwise sensible people post overly revealing videos and comments, often with the best of intentions. Many social media users point to a legitimate need to promote their work, and especially among wellness professionals, their explanation for oversharing is often altruistic. Users hope their openness about personal challenges will encourage followers to be more open with their own. The self-serving shadow side to this seemingly altruistic motivation is obvious and is dwarfed by the self-serving shadow side of the platforms themselves. Social media platforms were designed to create and reinforce habits to hook users, and there is ample and growing evidence that hooking their users causes significant harm, especially to teenagers who are in a critical phase of brain development. While social media has a positive side of giving people a forum to connect with others and express themselves, a growing number of studies link the frequency of social media use to teen depression and self-harm. The increase in these and other mental health issues directly coincides with when smartphone use became the norm among teens and their parents.[4]

Earlier, we saw that brains evolved to maximize our chances for survival so we can have children. Human connection leads to reproduction, so it makes sense that our brains reward it. Emojis, comments, and reposts on social media feel like human connection, even though they don't lead to survival or reproduction as directly as engaging with someone in person. Yet, the reward centers in our brains often equate the two. When we're pleased that people are engaging with our social media posts, our brains' reward centers flood our systems with dopamine. Dopamine is sometimes called the "feel-good" hormone, and feeling good motivates us to repeat the behavior. In effect, engagement on social media encourages us to climb on the hedonic treadmill and stay there. That's how social media platforms hook us. Attention plays an essential role in breaking unproductive habits like being hooked on social media and getting us off the hedonic treadmill. How do we do it?

....

Ignore the cue, interrupt the habit loop,
or reframe the reward.

....

Look at a map of Michigan, and you'll see two peninsulas surrounded by four of the five freshwater lakes called "The Great Lakes":[5] Lake Huron, Lake Superior, Lake Michigan, and Lake Erie. Plopped down between the two peninsulas in the Straits of Mackinac is Mackinac Island, a historical landmark known for a Victorian-era grand hotel; car-free streets plied by horse-drawn carriages; Fort Mackinac, a lovingly preserved military outpost built by the British in 1780; and rich, tasty fudge. Every summer when I was growing up, our family of five would pack a cooler with sandwiches and sodas and climb into my mom's station wagon to embark on an almost twelve-hour drive from the southwestern corner of the Lower Peninsula of Michigan to the northeastern tip of the Upper Peninsula (the UP). Midway was the Mackinac Bridge, a five-mile-long suspension bridge built in 1957, then the longest suspension bridge in the world. (Now the fifth longest.)

About twenty-five miles before we got to the bridge, we'd start seeing billboard after billboard enticing us to visit Mackinac Island and sample its world-famous fudge. Determined to make the drive in a single day and proud of it, my dad did not succumb to the temptation to stop—except for one October when I was a teenager and it was my birthday weekend. To celebrate, he and I drove to the UP on our own to see Michigan's magnificent fall colors at their peak. Halfway through the long drive, my dad stopped in Mackinaw City, and we took the ferry to Mackinac Island. I was a fan of horseback rides, and he had arranged for me to take one as a birthday surprise. The four-or-so-mile trail ride was slow and leisurely until my horse caught sight of the barn on the way back. Then, the expression "like a horse headed back to the barn" became more than a cliché as she sped up to a trot and wanted to gallop. It was all I could do to keep her from bolting.

I thought about that trail ride the first time I heard our minds and bodies compared to a horse and its rider; the horse as the body and the rider as the mind. There are many ways teachers use this analogy from Tibetan Buddhism to illustrate a simple truth that we've talked about before—our minds change our bodies, and our bodies change our minds. A skittish horse can make the rider skittish, and a steady horse can calm the rider. The opposite is true, too. A skittish rider can make the horse skittish, while a grounded, steady rider can calm the horse. I acted out the horse and rider analogy on that Mackinac Island trail ride. The barn was an environmental cue that triggered the release of dopamine in the horse's brain to start a behavioral habit loop—cue (barn), routine (speed up), reward (getting back to the comforts of the barn). The anticipation of returning to the barn got the horse moving, and the habit loop started to run. Before the trail ride began the guide had coached me through what to do if the horse bolted: tighten the reins, sit up in the saddle, and press your knees into her ribs. Following these instructions, I interrupted the habit loop and slowed down the horse. Like the horse, all of us have habits that aren't helpful. Whether we can effectively interrupt an unhelpful habit once it starts to run hinges on our level of awareness.

Conventional wisdom says that the cue triggers the habit loop, but there's more to it than that. Not to split hairs, but when we look closely at a habit loop, our awareness of the cue triggers the loop, not the cue itself. We must notice a cue to act on it. For a habit to run, awareness matters at the beginning of the loop. That's the point of habitual behavior—the routine runs automatically. Once we're aware of the cue (consciously or unconsciously), an automatically generated routine will bypass our conscious awareness so we can reliably respond to familiar situations without forming an intention or thinking something through. That awareness matters only at the start of a habit loop is more than just an efficient strategy when the routine is helpful; it's a necessary one. If we didn't have beneficial mental habits, our brains would become overloaded by routine tasks and shut down. But when trying to break or change an unhelpful habit, awareness matters at every point along the way—when we recognize the cue, feel the dopamine effect, enact the routine, and get the reward.

Earlier we saw that a stimulus and its response are often entangled so tightly that they seem to happen simultaneously. The same is true with deeply entrenched habits, especially emotional ones, where the habit loop runs so quickly that it feels like the cue, routine, and reward occur at once. The three elements of the loop are often tangled together like a knot and seem indistinguishable from one another. We can tease them apart by bringing awareness to each element.

....

When we bring awareness to the cue, we can consider strategies to stop it from triggering the routine.

....

Bringing awareness to the routine is an opportunity to see that, like everything else, habits are made up of multiple elements that depend on one another and change. Each of those changing, interdependent elements is an opportunity to interrupt the habit and alter its course.

....

When we bring awareness to the reward, we recognize that it's not a shift in our external circumstances that we're looking for—like a new rug for the bedroom or a promotion at work. The rug or the promotion is a means to an end. The end we seek is not outside us, but within us; we're looking for a positive shift in our internal state. If getting a new rug or a promotion doesn't make us feel better, at least for an instant, it's not a reward.

....

As we become aware of the many changing and interdependent elements at each stage in the habit loop, we're presented with countless opportunities to undermine the habit.

One thing to remember when working with habits: immediate satisfaction generally trumps delayed gratification. "The marshmallow test" is shorthand for a set of psychological studies conducted at Stanford University in the 1970s where Walter Mischel, Ebbe B. Ebbesen, and their colleagues ran a series of experiments that studied delayed gratification with preschool-aged children. The best known of these studies is the marshmallow test. Children were offered a choice: they could eat one marshmallow now or two marshmallows later. Most children didn't wait. In follow-up studies, researchers found that measures of health, happiness, and success in later life were higher in the children who were able to delay gratification than those who ate the marshmallow right away. Recent studies have been unable to replicate these findings. To the contrary, some studies have shown no correlation between someone's behavior later in life and whether they could wait to eat a marshmallow when they were in preschool.[6] That the results of the marshmallow test study have been called into question doesn't lessen the value of resisting temptation to get something better later, though. Is the moral of this story that delayed gratification is harder than immediate satisfaction, but it pays off in the end? Yes, but in the context of making, breaking, and changing habits, there's also a more targeted takeaway. To borrow from James Clear and his book *Atomic Habits*:

> Thankfully, it's possible to train yourself to delay gratification—but you need to work with the grain of human nature, not against it. The best way to do this is to add a little bit of immediate pleasure to the habits that pay off in the long run and a little bit of immediate pain to the ones that don't.[7]

Bringing kind, curious awareness to our habits can keep an engaged mind active for a long time. The amount of information entangled in our patterns about what motivates us and how we relate to the world is immeasurable. By bringing awareness to what we learn when we pay attention to our habits, we start a process of change and growth that can loosen the grip that unhelpful ones have on us, provided we pay attention with kindness.[8] Beating ourselves up when we notice the patterns that steer us away from the direction we want to go is counterproductive. Viewing these unhelpful habits as an invitation to practice self-compassion instead is an opportunity to practice treating ourselves with the same kindness, concern, and understanding that we would treat a dear friend.

Tsoknyi Rinpoche demonstrates how to kindly (and jokingly) interrupt patterned behavior by silently talking to our bodies and minds like they're a horse and its rider. He uses endearing terms when talking about patterned behavior, which brings a light touch to inner work that is sometimes heavy and upsetting. Here's an example of how I recently used Rinpoche's method with a deeply entrenched sugar habit I'm trying to break. I ran into the deli to grab a sandwich for lunch. While waiting in line at the deli counter, I felt a dopamine spike of pleasure when I noticed a package of my favorite cookies on the shelf next to me. I reached for them automatically before I remembered that I was trying to break my sugar habit. I stopped reaching for them and started thinking about something else. When I caught myself going for them again, I remembered Rinpoche's method and silently said something like this: "Thank you, dopamine, my dear horse, for taking such good care of me. You've been working hard to satisfy my sweet tooth for a long time. But I don't want to eat sweets anymore; they're not good for you, dear horse, or for me. Please take a well-earned rest and trust me to break this bad habit for both of us."

I felt a little silly, but the strategy had worked. I still love to eat cookies, but I wasn't craving this one anymore. There was something else, too: I noticed that I was smiling.

WRAP-UP: Awareness and Kindness

We are creatures of behavioral habits and emotional patterns. Once a habit is established, we repeat it effortlessly in response to familiar cues. When behavioral habits and emotional patterns align with our priorities and run automatically—outside our awareness—they free up energy and attention to focus on novel experiences and ideas. When they don't align with our priorities, they get in the way of growth and often set us back. That's why it makes sense to dig deep to look at what matters most to you before trying to break or change your habits. "Rowing harder doesn't help if the boat is headed in the wrong direction" is a remarkably relevant observation from Japanese organizational theorist Kenichi Ohmae that applies to everything, including habits.[9] First, we identify our priorities. That's awareness. Now, we have a benchmark against which to measure our habits, and then, with kindness and a sense of humor, we can determine whether we're rowing in the direction we want to go. If our habits are steering us in the wrong direction, we can correct our course.

Practice

Find a comfortable place where you won't be disturbed and take time to settle. Close your eyes if you like. If you keep them open, softly gaze downward or at a fixed point ahead of you. Without blocking your thoughts or feelings, allow your mind to be open and aware. When you're ready, reflect on the question, "What matters most?" Don't worry if answers don't come right away, just rest with the question. Stay with the question for as long as you can without getting lost. It's natural to become distracted. If that happens, focus on a sensation or sound until your attention stabilizes. When it stabilizes, return to the inquiry, "What matters most?"

When you are finished meditating, take a piece of paper, and draw a diagram with three concentric circles. Jot down your top priorities in the inner circle, write the things that matter but aren't your top priority in the middle circle, and put what matters least in the outer circle. Take a last look at the contents of the innermost circle. Is that what matters most to you right now?

Save the diagram and put it aside for later. If this practice feels familiar, it's because we've drawn similar diagrams before. We'll revisit these concentric circles diagrams in the chapter "What Matters Most?"

Takeaway

Notice the habits that take you away from what matters most to you and which ones take you toward it. If you're rowing in the wrong direction, how might you correct your course?

17

Everything Is in Play

Identity and the Myth of Perfection

"No one asked Susan" (slightly different in tone and meaning than "No one asked, Susan") is a four-word mantra I silently repeat to myself when I am about to offer unsolicited advice. It's from a story my grown daughter tells about a colleague who wrote that phrase on a sticky note (with the colleague's name, not mine) and posted it on his computer screen. On business calls, the colleague would offer more information than necessary, and the sticky note reminded him to hold back. I can say too much without thinking it through too and offer advice without being asked because "fixing things" has long been a core element of my identity. That started to change when I saw that my well-meaning and deeply entrenched habit of trying to fix other people's problems was not always welcome and could backfire. Many of the people who helped me realize this are from a twelve-step program called Al-Anon. Since I was a teenager, I've sat in church basements, community rooms, and, more recently, on Zoom meetings with people whose lives have been affected by a family member who struggles with alcohol or another addiction. I'm a dabbler when it comes to Al-Anon, though. I haven't gone the distance by getting a sponsor to work its twelve steps. Had I worked them, I might have responded differently in the story I am about to tell.

In the early 2000s, I cotaught a series of workshops for parents with Tom Nolan, then the dean of students at the Crossroads School in Santa Monica, California. The format of these workshops was Council, a practice that originated with indigenous cultures and was adapted for use in schools, communities, and businesses by the Ojai Foundation and others.[1] Using inquiry and storytelling as its primary methods, Council develops self-awareness, resolves conflict, and builds relationships. Inquiry is a participant-centered method that uses open-ended questions to examine Council members' principles, values, and core beliefs.[2] Members, not facilitators, drive the conversations by telling stories and asking questions that require them to think deeply about fundamental issues. Council promotes critical thinking, active listening, mutual respect, and respectful advocacy. It also nurtures humility by uncovering how we are connected to and dependent on one another in an ever-changing world. By reflecting on big-picture questions like "How do we explain the unexplainable, and why do we need an answer?" participants become more open to ambiguity and paradox.

Tom and I were not there to offer advice or give theoretical explanations. Like all Council facilitators, our role was to create a safe container for participants to understand their experiences through inquiry and storytelling and to help them navigate any big feelings or complex thoughts that bubbled up in the process. In an engaged Council practice, everyone's ideas, feelings, and habits are in play. Emotions are contagious. Few things are more rewarding to a facilitator than when someone unearths a meaningful insight and their positive experience ripples out into the group. Painful feelings also get unearthed, and they too are contagious. If not contained, they can spread like wildfire. Facilitators are not immune from emotional contagion, and part of their job is keeping their emotional baggage in check. I did a lousy job tracking and holding the emotional patterns that emerged in one of the Councils I led with Tom a long time ago—not the participants' emotional patterns, but my own. If I could do it again, I'd do it differently.

We set up the room in a circle with chairs and meditation cushions for people to sit on. Tom and I sat on the floor on one side of the circle, and when the participants arrived, we invited them to join us. Each session started with a period of silent meditation, and at this Council, a participant rushed in midway through the first meditation period. Seeming agitated, she took an empty chair and moved it into the circle. Following the Council format, we passed a ceremonial object called a talking piece. Sitting on my left, Tom had the talking piece and gave it to the person on his left. One by one, participants passed the talking piece and shared their feelings. I don't remember anyone saying anything unusual until the talking piece reached the last person in the circle. Being the last one to get the talking piece is only significant if someone wants to say something emotional and they've had to wait a long time to say it. Harold (not his real name) had listened to about twenty people before it was his turn to share. He had been holding in what he wanted to say for over half an hour.

Harold's hand was trembling when he took the talking piece. With a halting voice, Harold told us that he was conflicted and reluctant to speak up because the person who came in late had had a rough morning. Still, Harold was upset that she had taken his chair. Harold had a back injury and took the chair because he would need it later. He had planned to move from the floor to the chair when the meditation was through. Harold shared that usually he's afraid to defend himself and that allowing people to take advantage of him is a lifelong pattern he'd like to break. He believed that the only way for him to break the habit was to start speaking up.

In this Council, no cross talk was allowed the first time the talking piece was passed around the circle. That's a standard agreement that allows participants to speak without interruption. The effect of that ground rule was an awkward silence after Harold shared. He was uncomfortable. From where I sat, it looked like the person who came in late was also uncomfortable. I was too. For me, feeling other people's discomfort is like seeing the Bat-Signal from DC Comics' *Batman*: I want to swoop in like a superhero and save the day.

I thought I felt uncomfortable because the problem could have been solved quickly and easily. (Ultimately, I recognized that the roots of my discomfort were deeper.) When we set up the room, we thought people would choose to sit on a chair or cushion. There were empty chairs outside the circle, and I wondered why Harold didn't take one. Later, I learned that the chairs outside the circle had been claimed. Several participants had taken a cushion and a chair because they wanted something to lean against or sit on if the floor wasn't comfortable. Decades later, I still use the "chair incident" as shorthand for the remarkable number of life lessons that exemplify how everything is in play, especially in group dynamics. The chair signified something different for each of us. To Harold, the chair represented not taking care of himself; for me, it cued my "gotta fix this" habit; it meant something else for Tom and for the person who had mistakenly taken Harold's chair.

None of this should have affected the way I cofacilitated the group. Had I been at my best that day, I would have recognized my discomfort for what it was—my problem and my problem alone. But it was not my finest hour. While Tom was leading the group discussion, I quietly stood up, got one of the empty chairs, and brought it over to Harold. Like the person who was late and took Harold's chair without asking, I had taken someone else's chair without realizing it.

James Clear's book *Atomic Habits*, which we discussed in the previous chapter, offers a three-layered model of behavior change that connects habits with identity. Think of three concentric circles, like the three concentric circles of a wrapped Tootsie Pop with a chewy chocolate center. The outcome you get when you change your behavior is the outer layer—the wrapper over the Tootsie Pop. Processes, what you do to change behavior, are the middle layer—the hard candy under the wrapper. The core layer of behavior change—the chewy chocolate center—is identity. In *Atomic Habits*, Clear defines identity as your beliefs, worldview, self-image, and judgments about yourself and others.[3] Over two decades ago, when I was facilitating that parent Council with Tom, my sense of myself as someone whose job it was to fix problems was so deeply enmeshed in my core identity that it had become a habit that ran automatically. If I had recognized my "gotta fix this" habit, I could have tracked and contained it, but my identity as a fixer was so deep that I didn't see it that day. It's ironic that this habit emerged when it did because there's no fixing in Council practice, only healing. One of Council's core tenets is that participants heal themselves by telling their personal stories.

Typically, there are four hallmarks of emotional patterns that are tangled up with one another in a symbolic knot: one, we identify with them; two, we believe them to be accurate; three, our whole being is wrapped up in them—emotions, ideas, and senses—and four, all of them, like everything else, are in flux. My clumsy attempt to help Harold in that Council had all four characteristics.

> I mistakenly saw myself as someone who could fix Harold's problem (identity).
> I felt physically and emotionally uncomfortable doing nothing (whole-being involvement).
> I wrongly believed I could fix the problem, and (wrong again!) I thought it was my job to fix it (belief).
> Every step of the way, the dynamic changed. First, our emotions—Tom's, Harold's, the other participants', and my own. Then, our reactions—Tom's, Harold's, the other participants', and my own (all is in flux).

Now a new and more significant issue had emerged, and my misguided but well-meaning habit was poised to swoop back in to try and fix it. Fortunately, I had two things going for me: enough mindfulness to know that something was off and working with a friend and seasoned cofacilitator. Tom and I caught each other's eyes. I made a mental note to revisit all the above later— my identity, feelings, role, and beliefs—then, just like that, the discussion topic changed. We spent the rest of that parent Council unpacking what had happened.

The "chair incident" supports the provocative idea from two chapters back that we're wrong about everything. Because group dynamics are always filtered through individuals' perceptions that are based on incomplete information, it's impossible to see the whole picture. Without realizing it, our brains fill in the blanks with ideas based on past experiences which means that, in effect, we make everything up. In the chair incident, actions and reactions ricocheted off multiple patterns and perceptions (my own, Harold's, Tom's, and other people's) in a changing, interdependent process of group dynamics where everything was in play. I was reminded of the imperfections of perception and memory when I sent a draft of this chapter to others who had participated in the Council for their review and comment. They remembered the story's general arc, but each of us recalled the specifics a little differently.

This story has a silver lining: There's no such thing as a perfect facilitator, perfect spouse, perfect coworker, perfect parent, or perfect anyone. It's unrealistic to expect ourselves to be perfect.

....

The aim of mindfulness and meditation is
not to be perfect; it's to be present.

....

We notice when we're not at our best when we're present. Then, with mindful awareness, we can identify the right time and place to repair our mistakes through interpersonal connection.

"Golden repair" is a real thing and a charming metaphor for reframing mistakes. It's a method of fixing broken pottery developed in Japan five centuries ago called *kintsukuro* (literally, golden repair) or *kintsugi* (golden joinery). By filling cracks and gluing broken pottery together using lacquer with flakes of gold, platinum, or silver mixed into it, golden repair highlights the pottery's flaws instead of masking them. These glistening cracks serve as a reminder of the pottery's history. With ingenuity and a shift in perspective, what seems imperfect today becomes a treasure tomorrow. Here's my favorite fun fact about golden repair: once fixed, the pottery is sturdier and more resilient than before it was broken or cracked. What happened in this Council was an example of golden repair. I copped to having bungled the group facilitation; we talked about it as a group, and my having messed up proved to be the springboard for a meaningful conversation.

Meditation is an excellent place to become comfortable with the fact that we're imperfect humans who make mistakes. Watching the activity of our minds with compassion is an opportunity to see that wisdom doesn't come from being perfect; it comes from being present. This insight lets us abandon our expectations for what will happen when we practice. Instead of being hard on ourselves, we might watch what's happening in our minds with curiosity and a sense of humor. That in and of itself is an act of self-compassion and a call to humility. Can we then reframe the idea of perfection to view mistakes as opportunities to become stronger and more resilient?

WRAP-UP: Identity and the Myth of Perfection

Acknowledging interdependence, we recognize that countless factors are involved in every interaction. One of those factors is identity. By internalizing this perspective, we can stop hoping for perfection from ourselves or anyone else and give ourselves time to think three-dimensionally before reacting to group dynamics. By reserving judgment, we can step into another person's shoes to notice what we have in common and imagine how they feel. When we understand that perfection is a myth and emotional patterns are complex, especially as they relate to identity, we become more comfortable with the discomfort that can accompany fear, shame, anxiety, and the unknown.

Practice

Find a comfortable place to settle with paper and a pencil or pen. Relax, take a deep breath, hold it for a moment, then exhale. Breathe naturally for a few breaths while lightly focusing on your outbreath. Allow your mind to be open and aware without blocking your thoughts and feelings. Getting tangled up in thoughts and emotions is natural, but they don't need to carry you away. When you're ready, close your eyes (if they are open) and consider, "What aspects of my speech, actions, and relationships are part of my identity?" You might identify with being successful, creative, kind, fashionable, intelligent, funny, a hard worker, a big thinker, a good gardener, or a caregiver. Or you might identify with something else. You've done similar practices before.

Hold back from analyzing the ideas that surface and remember that reflecting on the question is more important than answering it. When you're ready, let go of the question and rest in open awareness. Then, open your eyes and jot down your thoughts. Draw three concentric circles on a piece of paper and consider which elements of your identity matter most. Jot those down in the center. What parts of your identity matter the least? Please place them in the outer ring. Everything else goes in between. In the next chapter, we'll revisit this diagram along with the three other concentric circle diagrams you made earlier.

Takeaway

Watch how various parts of your identity align with what you think, say, and do. What would happen if one or more aspect of your identity fell away? Would it matter? What would be left?

What Matters Most

Awareness and Discernment

"Taking time for what matters" was the original tagline for *Mindful* magazine, a social innovation initiative cofounded in 2012 by Jim Gimian and Barry Boyce, with the help and support of many others. It makes sense that these two pioneers in the movement to bring secular mindfulness into the mainstream would lead by encouraging us to prioritize how we spend our time. This chapter is designed to give readers an opportunity to follow their sage advice. To do so, we must clear a few hurdles.

The first hurdle is to find the time to identify our priorities. In four previous chapters, I asked you to reflect on various prompts and prioritize your answers. Then, I asked you to draw three concentric circles on a piece of paper and write down your answers in the order of their priority—highest in the center circle, lowest in the outer circle, and what's left in the circle in between. One goal of giving you these four prompts was to help you over the first hurdle and carve out time to reflect on issues that matter. Another goal was to give you a chance to get past the second hurdle and identify your priorities. If, like many busy readers, you didn't have a chance to consider the prompts before now, this is an opportunity to do so. The prompts were:

> What does it take for you to feel safe and welcome?
> What motivates you to do what you do?
> What do you want most for yourself and those you love?
> What aspects of your speech, actions, and relationships are
>   part of your identity?

To confidently identify what matters, you must also navigate a third hurdle. Recent psychological studies question how well you know yourself by asking, "Who is best equipped to spot what matters most to someone?" Perhaps your friends and colleagues are in a better position to identify what matters most to you. Why? Because what you *do* is often a better indication of your priorities than what you *say*. On the NPR podcast *Hidden Brain*, science journalist Shankar Vedantam spoke with a social psychologist from the University of Virginia, Tim Wilson, who explains:

> The people who know us well are good observers of our behavior, and they can deduce from our actions what we like and what we don't. And sometimes, we have theories ourselves that just go awry and don't match those preferences. So it's the people who are good observers of us who often can deduce our feelings better than we can.

Minutes later, Wilson continues:

Now, again, I don't want to exaggerate this. I don't mean to say we're clueless about how we feel, but I do think there are times when we get it wrong.[1]

Since finding a reliable answer to "What matters most?" can be elusive, the following practice is designed to help figure it out.

WRAP-UP: Awareness and Discernment

Discerning what matters most to us and becoming aware of whether our choices, speech, and actions line up with our core values are dynamic processes that evolve with new experiences and shifting circumstances. Navigating this shifting landscape is an essential step toward leading a less stressful and more meaningful life. When we are clear about our priorities, we can better set healthy boundaries, say no to nonessential commitments, and avoid spreading ourselves too thin. Clear priorities also guide us in setting meaningful, relevant goals that are aligned with our values and pursuing those goals skillfully.

While we are generally well-equipped to identify our priorities, others can sometimes tell what matters most to us better than we can. By observing whether our speech, actions, and priorities align, they can offer us insights into our patterns, behaviors, and choices. External, objective feedback helps us recognize that what we do, what we say, and how we spend our time can reflect what matters to us more accurately than our own assessment.

Practice

I promised we would revisit the concentric circle diagrams and now the time has come. Please review the four diagrams, looking for items that overlap. Then, create a new list with the items that repeat and note where you placed each repeating item on the diagram. One last time, draw three concentric circles on a piece of paper. Using only the items on the list you just created, reflect on the ones that matter most to you. Place the most important items in the center circle. Place the least important ones in the outer circle. Everything else goes in between. Consider your new diagram. Is it an accurate reflection of your priorities? Imagine what close friends or colleagues might say if they saw the diagram. Would they agree that the items you placed in the inner circle are what matter most to you?

Put aside your papers, pencils, pens, and diagrams.

Find a comfortable place to practice open awareness, and lightly rest your attention on your outbreath. Don't fight the thoughts and emotions that arise. With no goal or purpose, allow your mind to be open and rest.

Takeaway

Consider what you do and say today. If a year from now, you were to look back on how you spent your time, would you wish you had prioritized something else?

Conclusion: Try to Be Kinder[1]

Patience and Appreciation

My grown son had a middle seat on a cross-country flight between a family of three—dad on one side, mom on the other. The third family member was a restless and crying toddler and his parents passed him back and forth throughout the flight. When my son told me about his trip, he said, "Mom, I was traveling with the proverbial teaboy."

I first read the story of the renowned Indian teacher and scholar Atisha (whose work we considered earlier and who brought *The Seven Points of Training the Mind and Its 59 Slogans of Lojong* to Tibet) and the attendant who traveled with him in Pema Chödrön's book *The Places That Scare You*. Centuries ago, attendants like this one were called "teaboys." The story goes like this: Atisha brought a teaboy with him when he traveled to Tibet to give teachings. Atisha's teaboy was cranky, mischievous, and loud. He broke pottery and spilled the tea. Still, the esteemed monk took him everywhere. His hosts would say, "You must get rid of this teaboy. We'll help you find someone new." But Atisha refused, saying, "No, he is my greatest teacher. His very presence reminds me to be compassionate and gives me plenty of opportunities to practice patience."[2]

Everyone has proverbial teaboys in their life. One of my teaboys is a close friend who thinks the idea of real-world enlightenment is silly. Here are some overly simplistic versions of her concerns about enlightenment—a common definition of which is the uprooting of the three poisons we considered earlier of attachment, aggression, and ignorance (also called desire, anger, and delusion).

"If I need to uproot desire, anger, and delusion to become enlightened, count me out!"

"If it weren't for desire, I wouldn't get out of bed in the morning."

"Anger is an appropriate reaction to injustice. Uprooting it would be irresponsible."

"My hopes and dreams may be deluded, but they keep me going and on track."

"I want no part of enlightenment! It would even out the highs and lows in my life."

The Buddha's eightfold path to enlightenment is called the middle way for a reason, and my friend's arguments live in the extremes. Daily life is relative, and these three mental attitudes are viewed on a spectrum. They are seen as poisons when they manifest on either pole. When one of them displays as balanced—landing somewhere in the middle of the spectrum—it is seen as skillful. If this were a game of softball and my friend were the pitcher, statements like hers would be a fat pitch hanging over the plate. So why are these conversations of such value to me?

I will tell you.

My friend is one of the most intelligent people I know. Not only is she a successful artist, but she became one after abandoning a career as an American studies professor at a prestigious New England college. Wait, there's more. She attended Catholic school and was educated by Jesuits (known for their excellent debate training), and her hobby is philosophy. She doesn't just read philosophy. Over the pandemic, she taught an online course on the subject. For fun. So she is a more formidably intellectual sparring partner than I am accustomed to. I pay attention when she takes issue with something I say based on the insight and academic rigor she brings to the conversation. This is not to say she is always right. She is not always right. But her very engagement with my work encourages me to question everything. I'm grateful that she spurs me to think deeply. Our conversations can be exhausting and even destabilizing, but they are always worth the effort.

Friends, families, and colleagues aren't the only proverbial teaboys we manage. We also have inner teaboys—self-critical inner voices—which are remarkably creative at making us question ourselves. Without meaning to insult me, my friend sounds a lot like the teaboy in my head—the one that tells me I'm unsophisticated and act like I just fell off the back of a turnip truck, an image both metaphorical and literal in my case since I worked on an asparagus harvest crew when I was a teenager (not turnips, but close enough). Many have told me they also have a critical or controlling inner voice from their past narrating their lives. Some tell me that their inner teaboys speak to them in the harsh tone they were spoken to as a child. No one has ever told me that the voice in their head is a sweetheart.

We've seen that what we resist persists and that hoping to quiet our inner teaboys by arguing with them is ineffective at best. Might we meet our self-critical inner voice with love instead? Rarely are we as patient and compassionate with ourselves as we are with those dear to us. The harsh voice inside our head isn't a reflection of our best selves, but could it be coming from a place of goodness? Is our overly critical inner teaboy nothing more than a reflection of our wish to reach our highest potential?

Let's go back for a moment and reconsider our outer teaboys—like my friend the college professor turned artist. Might we look at the challenging people in our lives—our imperfect parents, friends, colleagues, partners, spouses, or ex-spouses—through the lens of goodness? Is the motivation for what they say and do simpler than we initially thought? Are they, at least in part, motivated by good intentions? *No(!)* might be the answer to one or more of these questions. But often the answer is *yes*. This doesn't excuse bad behavior or mean that we should spend time with toxic people, but it can make room for forgiveness.

Regardless of whether irksome teaboys are within or outside of us, it's helpful to reframe our reactions to them. When my inner heckler criticizes me, I remind myself that she's coming from my wish to be better and do better. When my friend disagrees with a position I take, I question it more deeply. Not because I feel unsophisticated, but because I recognize the limitations of my knowledge. Whatever I conclude, reconsidering my view deepens my understanding of the issue, and that wouldn't have happened if my friend hadn't questioned my assumptions. That alone is reason enough for me to be thankful, and it deftly illustrates the meaning behind the lojong slogan "Be grateful for everyone."

In the first few chapters of this book, we considered motivation and why people meditate. Setting goals for formal and informal meditation is tricky because meditators view the practice on two levels—a conventional one that helps us navigate daily life and an ultimate one where we let go of concepts like helpful and unhelpful to rest in the direct experience in the moment. Although we are encouraged to hold this goal lightly, the conventional approach aims to ease suffering through awareness. If we aren't careful, we can get sidetracked by zooming in too narrowly on the suffering we hope to reduce. Then our practice morphs into another flavor of striving, where we try to meet expectations to achieve certain ends. Striving is oriented toward the future, not the present. Given the changing nature of everything—outside pressures, expectations, outcomes, you name it—the goalposts will keep moving and the goal will stay out of reach.

By becoming comfortable with uncertainty and letting go of outcome-specific expectations, those who embody an ultimate view embrace looking for answers, but their contentment isn't predicated on finding one. Becoming comfortable with uncertainty isn't the same as giving up studying to learn what we don't know. Nor does letting go of certain expectations mean we give up trying to make the world a better place. If something is within our control and needs to be changed, we change it. But we let go of our preconceived ideas of what the outcome will be. Perhaps most importantly, it's essential we keep healthy personal boundaries when we let go of expectations. To borrow from Seth, "Let go of expectations, but don't be a chump." How? By being more like Winnie the Pooh, says Benjamin Hoff, author of *The Tao of Pooh*, "the most effortless bear we've ever seen."

"Just how do you do it, Pooh?" asks the narrator.

"Do what?" asked Pooh.

"Become so Effortless," says the narrator.

I don't do much of anything," says Pooh.

"But all those things of yours get done," replies the narrator.

"They just sort of happen," explains Pooh.

"Wait a minute. That reminds me of something from the Tao Te Ching." The narrator reaches for a book. "Here it is—chapter thirty-seven. Translated, it reads something like, 'Tao does not do, but nothing is not done.'

"That sounds like a Riddle," said Pooh.

The narrator replies, "It means that Tao doesn't force or interfere with things, but lets them work in their own way, to produce results naturally. Then whatever needs to be done is done."

"I see," said Pooh.[3]

Effortlessness is the key to embodying an ultimate view. Remember the Taoist principle wu wei, from the chapter on perfect action? Let's look at a real-world example. When you wade into a lake with your swim teacher, you have a goal: to learn to float. But the harder you struggle to float, the more likely you are to sink. You're more likely to stay on the surface of the water if you relax instead of trying harder. When you're relaxed, you're better able to respond wisely to what's happening within you (your thoughts, emotions, and sensations) and around you (other swimmers, the current, and the rocks or sharp objects that lie beneath the water's surface). Trying to understand wu wei intellectually can be mind-bending, but in practice it's as basic as you can get.

....

We only live one moment at a time.

....

I am pushing against a work deadline and stuck on how best to organize a challenging project. I know what I need to accomplish, but I don't know how. The law of diminishing returns has set in, and experience tells me to stop what I'm doing and walk outside. *Solvitur ambulando!* I put on my puffy down jacket and make for the door, my head swirling with thoughts. As I walk through the living room past the coffee table, a small blue vase with cut hyacinths catches my eye. I had bought them the day before at the bodega down the street from our apartment. The flowers were closed when I brought them home, but the small springtime perennials are in full bloom this morning. I'm quietly catapulted out of the morass in my head and into this very moment. I have never seen a magenta hyacinth before and am stunned by the color. Its reddish-purplish-pink flowers are magnificent. I point the hyacinths out to Seth, and we look at them together. Fully present at that moment, nothing is missing and all things connect. It feels like there's no separation between Seth, the hyacinths, and me. This is real-world enlightenment; there's no sense of "I" and no sense of "other." Everything we need to be happy and free is right here.

There are things we do just for the sake of doing them. Seth and I stopped what we were doing to marvel at the hyacinth and connect with its beauty and each other. Nothing else. We dance to dance, not to get anywhere. We listen to music for pleasure. We eat sweets because they taste good, not for their nutritional value. When we live life for its own sake, we are one step closer to enlightenment.

To lead a meaningful life takes patience, and patience comes when we internalize the universal themes explored in this book—especially the ones that remind us that we are part of nature and nature is part of us. Nobody is a solo actor unaffected by genetics, past experiences, current surroundings, and literally countless other factors. Since no one can know every cause and condition that leads up to this or any other moment, there is an element of uncertainty in absolutely everything. That I am here right now is a statistical improbability. The joint revelations that human knowledge is imperfect and that life is uncertain don't need to be scary; they can be liberating.

....

When we recognize that big feelings are ratcheting up our reactivity, we're free to ground ourselves in this very moment and let our thoughts and emotions be.

....

When we recognize that thoughts, emotions, and sensations are constantly changing, combining, and intermingling, we're free to disentangle ourselves from internal and external pressures.

....

When we recognize that we're free to stop fighting against the current and let go, we can bring the playfulness, attention, balance, and compassion that are inherent in each of us to daily life.

....

All it takes is patience. As in the well-known fable of the tortoise and the hare, while we're tempted to race to the finish line, going slowly and deliberately is often the fastest and most direct route to get where we want to go. Meditation is like that. With time, wise motivation, and strong teachers, we will see the size of the cloth— the enormity of suffering in the world. Then, being grateful for everyone and everything makes perfect sense, and trying to be kinder is what matters most.

How do we manage that?

In the old joke, someone asks a New York cabbie how to get to Carnegie Hall.

The answer: "Practice, practice, practice."

ACKNOWLEDGMENTS

Thanks to Beth Frankl, my editor at Shambhala Publications, for her excellent advice in shaping this book and her unwavering enthusiasm and support. Thanks to the rest of the Shambhala editorial team, especially Samantha Ripley and Ashley Benning.

An author is lucky to have a good editor, and I am beyond fortunate to have two of the best—Beth Frankl at Shambhala and developmental editor Barry Boyce. Barry has been a tremendous friend to the book and to me, as has my agent, Amy Rennert, whose patience and good cheer are unparalleled. Thank you.

Thanks to my dream team of early readers—Seth Greenland, of course, Tom Lutz, Cortland Dahl, Allegra Greenland, Gabe Greenland, John Romano, Billy Diamond, Nancy Forbes Romano, Drew Greenland, and Tom Nolan—for their suggestions and sound council.

I do not doubt that I've learned as much from my clients, students, and co-teachers as they have from me, especially from Inner Kids' stalwarts and collaborators Laurie Cousins, Kelly Barron, Deb Walsh, Tandy Parks, Nada Ghaneian, Amy Spies,

Ellis Enlow, Paula Dashiell, Tina Doley Carlson, Eliko Ozeki, Annaka Harris, Casey Altman, and Diane Cyr. Thank you.

Thanks to the countless colleagues, students, teachers, clinicians, and friends who have participated in Inner Kids training and seminars since the early 2000s. Special thanks to Kelly Barron, who served as a collaborator and editor on the most recent Inner Kids training manual.

Thanks to my primary teacher, Mingyur Rinpoche, for his inspirational presence. In my volunteer work with his nonprofit organizations, Tergar International and Tergar Schools, I have tossed around many ideas about universal themes with friends and colleagues over the years. Thanks to Amy Roth, Kelly Petrie, Justin Kelley, Sandra Fernandez, and Wally Mikula for being invaluable conversation partners.

Thanks to my weekly sitting group—Maureen "Mo" O'Sullivan, Ann Buck, Diana Gould, Kerry Madden, and Dotti Albertine-- for their agendaless love.

Endless thanks to my kitchen cabinet—the one that quite literally sits around the kitchen table with me—Allegra Greenland, Gabe Greenland, and Seth Greenland. They are excellent company, and I could not have written this book without them.

NOTES

Introduction

1. For more on the exchange of goods and ideas along the trade routes known as the Silk Road, see "The Silk Road," National Geographic website, updated May 20, 2022, https://education.nationalgeographic.org/resource/silk-road; and Azim Nanji and Sarfaroz Niyozov, "The Silk Road: Crossroads and Encounters of Faiths," Smithsonian Folklife Festival, https://festival.si.edu/2002/the-silk-road/the-silk-road-crossroads-and-encounters-of-faith/smithsonian.

2. Jerome Bruner was an American psychologist and professor. In the mid-twentieth century he made meaningful contributions to the fields of cognitive psychology and learning. The term *golden threads* is often associated with his theory of spiral curricula. For more on Bruner, see "Jerome Bruner," Harvard University Department of Psychology, https://psychology.fas.harvard.edu/people/jerome-bruner.

3. This translation of the sage Padmasambhava's teaching is from Tulku Urgen Rinpoche, *As It Is*, Volume II: *Essential Teachings from the Dzogchen Perspective* (Hong Kong: Rang Jung Yshe Publications, 2004).

Chapter One: We Have What We Need to Be Free

1. For more on the three-week "safer-at-home order" issued by LA County director of public health Barbara Ferrer, see Christianna Silva, "'We Know We Are Asking A Lot.' Los Angeles County Announces New Stay-At-Home Order," NPR, November 28, 2020, https://www.npr.org/sections/coronavirus-live-updates/2020/11/28/939712661/we-know-we-are-asking-a-lot-los-angeles-county-announces-new-stay-at-home-order.

Chapter Two: Take Good Care

1. Dacher Keltner, *Born to Be Good: The Science of a Meaningful Life* (New York: W. W. Norton, 2009).

2. Naomi Shihab Nye, *Words Under the Words: Selected Poems* (Portland, OR: Eighth Mountain Press, 1995).

3. The source of the well-known and often misattributed maxim is described in "If Not Now, When? A Recent History of Hillel's Misattributed Maxim from Ivanka Trump to Ronald Reagan," *Tablet Magazine*, September 12, 2016, https://www.tabletmag.com/sections/news/articles/if-not-now-when-a-recent-history-of-hillels-misattributed-maxim-from-ivanka-trump-to-ronald-reagan.

4. Edward Espe Brown, *No Recipe: Cooking as a Spiritual Practice* (Louisville, CO: Sounds True, 2018).

Chapter Three: Looking to Feel Better

1. Peter Sedlmeier and Jan Theumer, "Why Do People Begin to Meditate and Why Do They Continue?" *Mindfulness* 11, no. 6 (2020): 1527–45, https://doi.org/10.1007/s12671-020-01367-w.

2. The direct reference paraphrased here is: "The basic idea here is straightforward: If one is instructed to observe the breath and be aware whether it is a long breath or a short breath, one needs to remember to do this, rather than forget after a minute, five minutes, 30 minutes, and so forth. . . . [In] the specific context in which the practice of

mindfulness is envisaged by ancient Buddhist texts, in remembering that one should remember the breath, one is remembering that one should be doing a meditation practice; in remembering that one should be doing a meditation practice, one is remembering that one is a Buddhist monk; in remembering that one is a Buddhist monk, one is remembering that one is trying to root out greed, hatred and delusion." Rupert Gethin, "On Some Definitions of Mindfulness," *Contemporary Buddhism* 12, no. 1 (2011): 263–79, https://doi.org/10.1080/14639947 .2011.564843.

3. Typically Buddhists talk of the "four noble truths," however, contemporary Buddhist writers and scholars are moving away from that phrase because the translation is misleading. It's not the truths that are noble; it's those who understand the truths who are noble, because they have gained insight. When translating the Sanskrit, Chatvari-arya-satyani (Pali: Chattari-ariya-saccani), *noble* (Sanskrit: *arya*; Pali: *ariya*) refers to those that understand the truths, not the truths themselves. Donald S. Lopez, *Four Noble Truths, Encyclopedia Britannica*, August 11, 2023, https://www.britannica.com/topic/Four -Noble-Truths.

4. Marie Kondo, *The Life-Saving Magic of Tidying Up: The Japanese Art of Decluttering and Organizing* (Berkeley, CA: Clarkson Potter/Ten Speed, 2014).

5. This translation is from "Renunciation," Rigpa Wiki, accessed October 5, 2023, https://www.rigpawiki.org/index.php?title=Renunciation.

6. The parable of the second arrow is from the Sallatha Sutta. This translation from the Pali is from "Sallatha Sutta: The Arrow" (SN 36.6), trans. Thanissaro Bhikku, *Access to Insight (BCBS edition)*, November 2013, https://www.accesstoinsight.org/tipitaka/sn/sn36 /sn36.006.than.html.

7. *Captain Fantastic*, written and directed by Matt Ross (Electric City Entertainment/Shiv Hans Pictures, 2016).

8. *The Office*, season 3, episode 5, "Initiation," directed by Randall Einhorn, written by B. J. Novak, aired October 19, 2006, on NBC.

Chapter Four: What Seekers Seek

1. Paul Bowles, *The Sheltering Sky* (Boulder, CO: Paladin, 1990), 13.
2. Tom Lutz, *Aimlessness* (New York: Columbia University Press, 2021), 123.
3. *The Big Lebowski*, written and directed by Joel and Ethan Coen (London: Working Title Films, 1998).
4. George Saunders, *A Swim in the Pond in the Rain: In Which Four Russians Give a Master Class on Writing, Reading, and Life* (New York: Random House Publishing Group, 2022), 157.
5. For more on the beneficial effects of nature on our minds and bodies, see Annie Murphy Paul, *The Extended Mind: The Power of Thinking Outside the Brain* (Boston: Houghton Mifflin Harcourt, 2021), 91–96.
6. Elissa Epel, *The STRESS Prescription: Seven Days to More Joy and Ease* (London: Penguin Publishing Group, 2022), 122.
7. Michael Pollan, *How to Change Your Mind: What the New Science of Psychedelics Teaches Us about Consciousness, Dying, Addiction, Depression, and Transcendence* (London: Penguin Publishing Group, 2019).
8. Milton Steinberg, *As a Driven Leaf* (Lanham, MD: J. Aronson, 1987).
9. Online Etymology Dictionary: Old English *giernan* (West Saxon), *geornan* (Mercian), *giorna* (Northumbrian) "to strive, be eager, desire, seek for, beg, demand," from Proto-Germanic *gernjan* (source also of Gothic *gairnjan* "to desire," German *begehren* "to desire"; Old High German *gern*, Old Norse *gjarn* "desirous," Old English *georn* "eager, desirous," German *gern* "gladly, willingly"), from PIE root *gher* "to like, want." *Etymonline—Online Etymology Dictionary*, https://www.etymonline.com.
10. The full statement from Saljay Rinpoche is: "Everyone is homesick because our true home is inside us, and until we recognize that, we will long for comfort outside ourselves." Yongey Mingyur Rinpoche with Helen Tworkov, *Turning Confusion into Clarity: A Guide to the Foundation Practices of Tibetan Buddhism* (Boston: Shambhala, 2014), 163.
11. Christopher Isherwood, *My Guru and His Disciple* (New York: Farrar, Straus and Giroux, 2013), 49.

12. For more on the Hubble and Webb Space Telescopes, see the website for NASA, https://www.nasa.gov.

13. The interviews with Leonard Cohen that are cited here can be found at one hour and thirty-three minutes to one hour and thirty-five minutes in the documentary *Hallelujah: Leonard Cohen, A Journey, A Song*, written and directed by Daniel Geller and Dayn Goldfine; performances by Leonard Cohen, Nancy Bacal, and Steve Berkowitz (Sony Pictures Classics, 2021).

14. Yasmin Anwar, "Ooh là là! Music evokes at least 13 emotions. Scientists have mapped them," *Berkeley News*, January 16, 2020, https://news.berkeley.edu/2020/01/06/ooh-l-l-music-evokes-at -least-13-emotions-scientists-have-mapped-them.

Chapter Five: For Everyone and Everything

1. The full tweet reads: "Being judgmental is not about how quickly you form opinions. It's how certain you are of them. Strong convictions from weak info reflect arrogance. Holding views lightly and revising them rapidly reveals humility. Wisdom often ends in a question mark, not an exclamation point." It can be found here (accessed October 5, 2023): https://twitter.com/AdamMGrant /status/1559563948831162368.

2. Dalai Lama, *The Middle Way: Faith Grounded in Reason* (Boston: Wisdom Publications, 2009), 136.

3. You can read the full transcript of Ezra Klein's podcast with Rick Rubin here: "Ezra Klein Interviews Rick Rubin," *New York Times*, February 10, 2023, https://www.nytimes.com/2023/02/10/podcasts /ezra-klein-show-transcript-rick-rubin.html.

Chapter Six: Survival 2.0

1. Alyssa Hui, "How Does Stress Manifest in the Body?" Verywell Health, April 5, 2023, https://www.verywellhealth.com/how-does -stress-affect-different-parts-of-the-body-7375233.

2. The two songs about the shadow side of romantic love referenced in this chapter can be found on YouTube here: "Love Is Just a Four-Letter

Word," song by Bob Dylan, vocals by Joan Baez, https://music
.youtube.com/watch?v=g1fpDWXwfso, and "Love's a Loaded
Word," song by Gene Clark, Pat Robinson, and Nicky Hopkins,
vocals by Pat Robinson, performed by The Byrds, https://music.
youtube.com/watch?v=RU1VOqi5M6M.

3. Homer, *The Iliad*, trans. Robert Fagles (London: Penguin Publishing
   Group, 1990), 14:257–61.

4. Leo Tolstoy, *War and Peace*, trans. Richard Pevear and Larissa
   Volokhonsky (New York: Vintage, 2011), 921.

5. Alan Watts, *The Wisdom of Insecurity: A Message for an Age of Anxiety*
   (New York: Knopf Doubleday Publishing Group, 1951), 130.

6. Annie Murphy Paul, *The Extended Mind: The Power of Thinking
   Outside the Brain* (Boston: Houghton Mifflin Harcourt, 2021), 60.

7. Yongey Mingyur Rinpoche with Helen Tworkov, *Turning Confusion
   into Clarity: A Guide to the Foundation Practices of Tibetan Buddhism*
   (Boston: Shambhala, 2014), 189.

Chapter Seven: Don't Think about a White Bear

1. For more on the myth that our problem-solving minds run the show, see
   Robert Wright, *Why Buddhism Is True: The Science and Philosophy of
   Meditation and Enlightenment* (New York: Simon and Schuster, 2017).

2. Wegner calls this thought experiment "Don't Think about a White
   Bear." Daniel Wegner and David Schneider, "The White Bear Story,"
   Psychological Inquiry 14, no. 3/4 (2003): 326–29, http://www.jstor
   .org/stable/1449696.

3. Christopher Germer, *The Mindful Path to Self-Compassion: Freeing
   Yourself from Destructive Thoughts and Emotions* (New York: Guilford
   Publications, 2009), 33.

4. Wright, *Why Buddhism Is True*, 32.

5. Kristin Neff, *Fierce Self-Compassion: How Women Can Harness
   Kindness to Speak Up, Claim Their Power, and Thrive* (New York:
   HarperCollins, 2021).

6. For more on how gratitude benefits relationships, see Sara B. Algoe,

Barbara L. Fredrickson, and Shelly L. Gable, "The Social Functions of the Emotion of Gratitude via Expression," *Emotion* 13, no. 4 (2013): 605–9, https://doi.org/10.1037/a0032701.

Chapter Eight: The Just-Right-for-Me Rule

1. To find out more about Vygotsky's zone of proximal development in education, see Alex Kozulin, Boris Gindis, Vladimir Ageyev, and Suzanne Miller (eds.), *Vygotsky's Educational Theory in Cultural Context* (Cambridge: Cambridge University Press, 2003), https://doi.org/10.1017/CBO9780511840975.

2. Pema Chödrön, *Welcoming the Unwelcome: Wholehearted Living in a Brokenhearted World* (Boulder, CO: Shambhala, 2020), 58–60.

3. Ruth King's Mindful of Race training program is based on her excellent book *Mindful of Race: Transforming Racism from the Inside Out* (Louisville, CO: Sounds True, 2018).

4. Tuckman initially described four main stages of team development: Forming, Storming, Norming, and Performing. Later, he added a fifth stage: Adjourning/Transforming. Bruce Tuckman, "Developmental sequence in small groups," *Psychological Bulletin* 63, no. 6 (1965): 384–99, https://doi.org/10.1037/h0022100; Debra Patterson, "4.6. In-depth Look: Tuckman's Model – Five Stages of Team Development," in *Strategic Project Management: Theory and Practice for Human Resource Professionals* (Pressbooks, 2022), https://ecampusontario.pressbooks.pub/hrstrategicprojectmanagementtheory/chapter/4-6-in-depth-look-tuckmans-model-five-stages-of-team-development.

5. *Annie Hall*, directed by Woody Allen, written by Woody Allen and Marshall Brickman (UnitedArtists, 1977).

6. For more on Tsoknyi Rinpoche's teaching "real but not true," see his book *Open Heart, Open Mind: Awakening the Power of Essence Love* (New York: Harmony/Rodale, 2012).

7. Brené Brown, *Daring Greatly: How the Courage to Be Vulnerable Transforms the Way We Live, Love, Parent, and Lead* (London: Penguin Publishing Group, 2015).

Chapter Nine: Our Bodies and Surroundings Change Minds

1. Bob Kaylor, "Solvitur ambulando," transcript of sermon, accessed October 6, 2023, https://bobkaylor.com/solvitur-ambulando.

2. For more on Hippocrates and the true origin of popular quotes attributed to him see Helen King, *Hippocrates Now: The "Father of Medicine" in the Internet Age* (London: Bloomsbury Academic, 2021). She looks at the quote "Walking is the best medicine" on pages 105–10.

3. *Encyclopedia Britannica Online*, s.v. "Lyceum," accessed October 6, 2023, https://www.britannica.com/topic/Lyceum-Greek-philosophical-school.

4. Friedrich Nietzsche, *Twilight of the Idols* (Oxford, UK: OUP Oxford: Oxford University Press, 2008).

5. Søren Kierkegaard, *Kiekegaard's Writings: Letters and Documents*, trans. Henrik Rosenmeier (Princeton, NJ: Princeton University Press), 25:214–15.

6. Carole Cadwalladr, "Frédéric Gros: Why going for a walk is the best way to free your mind," *Guardian*, April 19, 2014, https://www.theguardian.com/books/2014/apr/20/frederic-gros-walk-nietzsche-kant.

7. For more on mobility problems in the United States, see Lisa I. Iezzoni, Ellen P. McCarthy, Roger B. Davis, and Hilary Siebens, "Mobility difficulties are not only a problem of old age," *Journal of General Internal Medicine* 16, no. 4 (April 2001): 235–43, doi: 10.1046/j.1525-1497.2001.016004235.x. PMID: 11318924; PMCID: PMC1495195.

8. Henry David Thoreau, *Walking* (Cambridge, MA: Riverside Press, 1914).

9. Linnie Marsh Wolfe (ed.), *John of the Mountains: The Unpublished Journals of John Muir* (Madison, WI: University of Wisconsin Press, 1979).

10. *Grey's Anatomy*, season 11, episode 14, "The Distance," directed by Eric Laneuville, written by Shonda Rhimes and Austin Guzman, originally aired on March 4, 2015, on ABC.

11. Kim Elsesser, "The Debate on Power Posing Continues: Here's Where

We Stand," *Forbes*, October 2, 2020, https://www.forbes.com/sites
/kimelsesser/2020/10/02/the-debate-on-power-posing-continues
-heres-where-we-stand/?sh=48af1e3202ee.

12. For more on Amy Cuddy's power posing study, see "The most popular
TED Talks of all time," TED.com, https://www.ted.com/playlists
/171/the_most_popular_talks_of_all; Elsesser, "The Debate on Power
Posing Continues"; Susan Dominus, "When the Revolution Came for
Amy Cuddy," *New York Times*, October 18, 2017, https
://www.nytimes.com/2017/10/18/magazine/when-the-revolution
-came-for-amy-cuddy.html.

13. Annie Murphy Paul, *The Extended Mind: The Power of Thinking
outside the Brain* (Boston: Houghton Mifflin Harcourt, 2021), 92.

14. For more on how our surroundings change our minds, see Paul, *The
Extended Mind*; Esther Sternberg, *Healing Spaces: The Science of Place
and Well-Being* (Cambridge, MA: Harvard University Press, 2009);
"Building Community and Connection in an Age of Isolation,"
Newport Institute, December 13, 2021, https://www.newportinstitute
.com/resources/treatment/building-community.

15. Satchin Panda, *The Circadian Code: Lose Weight, Supercharge Your
Energy, and Transform Your Health from Morning to Midnight* (New
York: Harmony/Rodale, 2020), 13.

16. Rosie Blau, "The light therapeutic," *Economist*, December 29, 2014,
https://www.economist.com/1843/2014/12/29/the-light-therapeutic.

17. For more on the connection between our biological clocks and natural
or artificial light, see Panda, *The Circadian Code*; Satchin Panda, "A
healthy circadian rhythm may keep you sane and increase resilience to
fight COVID-19," University of California, April 9, 2020, https://www
.universityofcalifornia.edu/news/healthy-circadian-rhythm-may-keep
-you-sane-and-increase-resilience-fight-covid-19; Blau, "The light
therapeutic"; Hanae Armitage, "Ask Me Anything: Neuroscience with
Andrew Huberman," Scope blog, Stanford Medicine, October 5, 2022,
https://scopeblog.stanford.edu/2022/10/05/ask-me-anything-neuro
science-with-andrew-huberman.

Chapter Ten: Steady like a Log

1. Dza Kilung Rinpoche, *The Relaxed Mind* (Boulder, CO: Shambhala, 2015), 22–23.

2. The English translation of these three stanzas is from Pema Chödrön, *No Time to Lose: A Timely Guide to the Way of the Bodhisattva* (Boston: Shambhala, 2007).

3. For more on *The Seven Points of Training the Mind and Its 59 Slogans of Lojong*, see Norman Fischer, *Training in Compassion: Zen Teachings on the Practice of Lojong* (Boston: Shambhala, 2013); "Tonglen Lojong with Acharya Judy Lief," *Tricycle: The Buddhist Review*, June 11, 2010, https://tricycle.org/article/tonglen-lojong-acharya-judy-lief.

4. Reggie Ray, *Secret of the Vajra World: The Tantric Buddhism of Tibet* (Boston: Shambhala, 2002), 76.

5. For more on the "heavier-handed" meditation method called "crushing mind with mind itself," see *Vitakkasanthana Sutta: The Relaxation of Thoughts*, trans. Thanissaro Bhikku: "A fifth way to relax thoughts, if after trying the first four methods unskillful thoughts still arise, try "crushing [your] mind with awareness." Accessed October 6, 2023, https://www.accesstoinsight.org/tipitaka/mn/mn.020.than.html.

Chapter Eleven: So Be It

1. Rainer Maria Rilke, *Book of Hours: Love Poems to God* (London: Penguin Publishing Group, 2005).

2. Andy Karr, *Contemplating Reality: A Practitioner's Guide to the View in Indo-Tibetan Buddhism* (Boston: Shambhala, 2007), Kindle location 2756.

3. Tsoknyi Rinpoche, "How to Drop into Your Body and Feelings," *Lion's Roar*, January 15, 2022, https://www.lionsroar.com/how-to-drop-into-your-body-feelings/.

Chapter Twelve: Perfect Action

1. Thomas Merton, *The Way of Chuang Tzu* (second edition) (New York: New Directions, 2010), 28.

2. Benjamin Hoff, *The Tao of Pooh* (London: Penguin Books, 1983), 54.

Chapter Thirteen: What Will You Do in the Bardo?

1. The title of this chapter is a nod to the book by Yongey Mingyur Rinpoche with Helen Tworkov, *In Love with the World: A Monk's Journey through the Bardos of Living and Dying* (New York: Random House Publishing Group, 2021), 48 (story of brother moving to Kathmandu).

2. Christof Koch, "What Near-Death Experiences Reveal about the Brain," *Scientific American*, June 1, 2020, https://www.scientific american.com/article/what-near-death-experiences-reveal-about -the-brain.

3. Koch, "What Near-Death Experiences Reveal about the Brain."

4. Gideon Lichfield, "The Science of Near-Death Experiences," *The Atlantic*, April 2015, https://www.theatlantic.com/magazine/archive /2015/04/the-science-of-near-death-experiences/386231.

5. Mingyur Rinpoche and Tworkov, *In Love with the World*, 51. See this title for more on the classical bardo stages in Tibetan Buddhism.

6. Pema Chödrön, *Living Beautifully: With Uncertainty and Change* (Boulder, CO: Shambhala, 2019), 48.

7. F. Scott Figzgerald, *The Crack-Up* (New York: New Directions, 2009). The original *Esquire* essay is also reprinted on the PBS American Masters website page, August 31, 2005, https://www.pbs.org/wnet /americanmasters/f-scott-fitzgerald-essay-the-crack-up/1028.

8. Stephen Hebron, "John Keats and 'negative capability,'" British Library website, May 15, 2014, https://www.bl.uk/romantics-and-victorians /articles/john-keats-and-negative-capability.

9. Bertrand Russell, *A History of Western Philosophy: Collectors Edition* (London: Taylor and Francis, 2013), 92.

10. Ed Yong, *An Immense World: How Animal Senses Reveal the Hidden Realms around Us* (New York: Random House Publishing Group, 2022), 13.

11. Jonny Thomson post, Philosophyminis Instagram account, March 4, 2023, https://www.instagram.com/p/CpXmrQCouYO. For more from Jonny Thomson, see *Mini Philosophy: A Small Book of Big Ideas* (London: Headline Publishing Group, 2021).

Chapter Fourteen: The Stories We Tell Ourselves

1. This quotation is actually a paraphrase of Frankl's views as told by Stephen Covey. From viktorfrankl.org: "The true origin of the quotation is somewhat involved. To put it shortly, the author Stephen R. Covey used to recount that he found the quote in a library book and thought it fitting to describe Frankl's views, but he did not note down the book's author and title."

2. For more on the brain and its autopilot mode, Jessica Hamzelou, "Your autopilot mode is real - now we know how the brain does it," *New Scientist*, October 23, 2017, https://www.newscientist.com/article/2151137-your-autopilot-mode-is-real-now-we-know-how-the-brain-does-it.

3. I don't know who first used the term *add-on* in this context. I first heard it from Joseph Goldstein, a highly esteemed American meditation teacher who co-founded the Insight Meditation Society in Barre, Massachusetts.

Chapter Fifteen: We're Wrong about Everything

1. *The Crown*, season 5, episode 5, "The Way Ahead," directed by May el-Toukhy, written by Peter Morgan, Meriel Baistow-Clare, and Daniel Marc Janes, aired on November 9, 2022, on Netflix.

2. Mark Manson, *The Subtle Art of Not Giving a F*ck: A Counterintuitive Approach to Living a Good Life* (New York: HarperCollins, 2016), chapter 6.

3. For more on how our brains act as prediction machines, see: Anil Ananthawamy, "To Be Energy-Efficient, Brains Predict Their Perceptions," *Quanta Magazine*, November 15, 2021, https://www.quantamagazine.org/to-be-energy-efficient-brains-predict-their-perceptions-20211115.

4. Tarthang Tulku, *Revelations of Mind: An Experiential Inquiry into Mind, Self, and Reality* (Berkeley, CA: Dharma Publishing, 2013), 2.

5. To read David J. Linden's full essay, see "A Neuroscientist Prepares for Death: Lessons my terminal cancer has taught me about the mind,"

The Atlantic, December 30, 2021, https://www.theatlantic.com/ideas
/archive/2021/12/terminal-cancer-neuroscientist-prepares-death
/621114.

6. Alan Watts, *The Wisdom of Insecurity: A Message for an Age of Anxiety*
(New York: Knopf Doubleday Publishing Group, 1951), 10.

7. The Two Wolves story is a well-known parable, the origin of which
is uncertain. It is usually attributed to Native American origins, but
sources indicate that the origin of the story may be Christian. See
âpihtawikosisân, "Check the tag on that 'Indian' story," *âpihtawikosisân:
Law, Language, Culture* (blog), February 21, 2012, https://apihta
wikosisan.com/2012/02/check-the-tag-on-that-indian-story.

8. While this statement is commonly attributed to Rabbi Zalman
Schachter-Shalomi, a prominent figure in Jewish Renewal and
a pioneer in the field of Jewish spirituality, the exact source or
publication where it originated is unclear. Author and spiritual teacher
Sylvia Boorstein is also widely acknowledged for comparing minds
to tofu saying, "The mind is like tofu: it tastes like whatever it is
marinated in." The exact source or publication where this statement
originated is also unclear.

9. Naomi Shihab Nye, *Words Under the Words: Selected Poems* (Portland,
OR: Eighth Mountain Press, 1995).

Chapter Sixteen: Nobody Is Running the Show—The Habits Chapter

1. Charles Duhigg, *The Power of Habit: Why We Do What We Do in Life
and Business* (New York: Random House Publishing Group, 2012),
preface.

2. For more on habits, see James Clear, *Atomic Habits: An Easy and
Proven Way to Build Good Habits and Break Bad Ones* (London:
Penguin Publishing Group, 2018); Duhigg, *The Power of Habit*;
Gretchen Rubin, *Better Than Before: What I Learned about Making
and Breaking Habits—To Sleep More, Quit Sugar, Procrastinate Less,
and Generally Build a Happier Life* (New York: Crown, 2015). For a
deep dive into mindful awareness as an essential element in unwinding
emotional habits, see Judson Brewer, *Unwinding Anxiety: New Science*

Shows How to Break the Cycles of Worry and Fear to Heal Your Mind (London: Penguin Publishing Group, 2022).

3. Maia Szalavitz, "Dopamine: The Currency of Desire," *Scientific American*, January 1, 2017, https://doi.org/10.1038/scientific americanmind0117-48.

4. For more on the shadow side of social media use and its adverse effects, see Office of Surgeon General, "Social Media and Youth Mental Health: The U.S. Surgeon General's Advisory / 2023," U.S. Department of Health and Human Services, https://www.hhs.gov/sites/default /files/sg-youth-mental-health-social-media-advisory.pdf; an analysis of over 84,000 people between 10 and 80 years old that shows a negative relationship between self-reported social media use and life satisfaction, especially among adolescents, see Amy Orben, Andrew K. Przybylski, Sarah-Jayne Blakemore, and Rogier A. Kievit, "Windows of developmental sensitivity to social media," *Nature Communications* 13, no. 1649 (2022), https://doi.org/10.1038/s41467-022-29296-3; Dr. Leana S. Wen, "Social Media is Devastating Teens' Mental Health. Here's What Parents Can Do," *Washington Post*, March 21, 2023, https://www.washingtonpost.com/opinions/2023/03/21/teens -social-media-mental-health; Dr. Leana S. Wen, "Yes, Social Media Use is Linked to Depression in Teens," *Washington Post*, March 23, 2023, https://www.washingtonpost.com/opinions/2023/03/23/teens -mental-health-social-media-depression-research; Tristan Harris, "TED Talk: How a handful of tech companies control billions of minds every day," YouTube, July 28, 2017, https://www.youtube.com /watch?v=C74amJRp730.

5. The Great Lakes are a group of five large freshwater lakes that hold nearly one-fifth of the freshwater on the Earth's surface. They are located primarily on the border between the United States and Canada. They are Lake Superior, Lake Michigan, Lake Huron, Lake Erie, and Lake Ontario. Michigan is the home to four of these five Great Lakes. "Michigan's Great Lakes," Pure Michigan, accessed August 29, 2023, www.michigan.org/great-lakes.

6. For more on the marshmallow test and how its findings have been called into question, see Dee Gill, "New Study Disavows the Marshmallow Test's Predictive Power," *UCLA Anderson Review*, February 24, 2021, https://anderson-review.ucla.edu/new-study -disavows-marshmallow-tests-predictive-powers; Athena Chan, "Culture Matters in 'Marshmallow Test, Experiment on Japanese, American Kids Shows," *International Business Times*, July 24, 2022, https://www.ibtimes.com/culture-matters-marshmallow-test -experiment-japanese-american-kids-shows-3584900.

7. Clear, *Atomic Habits*, 189.

8. For more on emotional patterns and how to use mindfulness to work with them skillfully, see Brewer, *Unwinding Anxiety*.

9. Kenichi Ohmae, quoted in William J. Brown, Hays W. McCormick III, and Scott W. Thomas, *AntiPatterns in Project Management* (Hoboken, NJ: Wiley, 2000).

Chapter Seventeen: Everything Is in Play

1. For more on Council practice, see Jack Zimmerman and Virginia Coyle, *The Way of Council* (New York: Bramble Books, 2009).

2. For more on inquiry as an educational method, see Elizabeth M. Ross, "Creating a Culture of Inquiry in Schools," Harvard Graduate School of Education website, April 27, 2023, https://www.gse.harvard.edu /news/uk/23/04/creating-culture-inquiry-schools.

3. James Clear, *Atomic Habits: An Easy and Proven Way to Build Good Habits and Break Bad Ones* (London: Penguin Publishing Group, 2018), chapter 2.

Chapter Eighteen: What Matters Most

1. Tim Wilson, "You 2.0: How to See Yourself Clearly," Hidden Brain Podcast, transcript from episode posted on August 8, 2022, https://hiddenbrain.org/podcast/you-2-0-how-to-see-yourself -clearly.

Conclusion: Try to Be Kinder

1. The chapter title "Try to Be Kinder" is a nod to "Congratulations, by the Way," a convocation address at Syracuse University given by George Saunders in 2013, which was later published as *Congratulations, by the Way: Some Thoughts on Kindness* (New York: Random House Publishing Group, 2014).

2. For more on the Indian sage Atisha and the story of the proverbial teaboy, see Pema Chödrön, *The Places That Scare You: A Guide to Fearlessness* (Boston: Shambhala, 2004), 46; Andy Karr, *Into the Mirror: A Buddhist Journey through Mind, Matter, and the Nature of Reality* (Boulder, CO: Shambhala, 2023), 168.

3. Benjamin Hoff, *The Tao of Pooh* (London: Penguin Books, 1983), 56.